PERITO MORENO'S TRAVEL JOURNAL

A PERSONAL REMINISCENCE

PERITO MORENO'S TRAVEL JOURNAL
A PERSONAL REMINISCENCE

COMPILED BY EDUARDO V. MORENO

el ELEFANTE
BLANCO

910.4   Moreno, Francisco P.
MOR   Perito Moreno's Travel Journal: A Personal Reminiscence
1ª ed. - Buenos Aires - El Elefante Blanco, 2002
240 p. ; 23 x 15 cm.

© de la traducción: Victoria Barcelona

ISBN: 987-9223-57-8

I. Título - 1. Relatos de viajes

EDICIONES EL ELEFANTE BLANCO

Directora: Marta Gallardo

1ª edición en castellano de El Elefante Blanco, marzo 1997
1ª reimpresión: agosto 1997
2ª reimpresión: diciembre 1999

© 2002, El Elefante Blanco
Posadas 1359 - (1011) Buenos Aires - Argentina
http://www.elefanteblanco.com

ISBN: 987-9223-57-8

Editado e impreso en la Argentina

DEDICATION

To all those who carried out my father's vision in Nahuel Huapi and in honor of those he memorializes in this book, which not only looks back on his own life, but also chronicles many forgotten chapters in the history of our beloved country.

Eduardo V. Moreno

"I take pride in knowing that I, among others,
was born to serve my country."

Francisco P. Moreno
(1852-1919)

PROLOGUE[1]

Remembering Francisco P. Moreno

"Pancho"* Moreno had a one-of-a-kind personality and it is indeed difficult to peg his character. Like two other national heroes, Bartolomé Mitre and Domingo F. Sarmiento, he was self-taught. In fact, Sarmiento once had to grant him an honorary doctorate degree by telegram in order to resolve an administrative matter.

Moreno was a gifted person who drew upon his own talents and nature to become a philosopher, a wise man, a philanthropist, and a poet, accomplishments that no amount of schooling could have provided. Pancho Moreno's style was unique. He was above all a man of action who translated his ideas into deeds. It would be wrong to judge him on anything but his track record.

His whole personality was focused upon action: He was single-minded, loyal and straightforward, though not devoid of an astounding degree of naiveté. He was honorable and his heart was in the right place, although at times he underestimated his own powerful momentum and became the *enfant terrible* that lies beneath all great men.

Moreno was solely known by his actions, while the motives behind those actions were often a mystery. He had an irresistible need to perform, to which he once nostalgically referred by stating, "As a child, I remember seeing a traveling musician in a poor section of Buenos Aires playing several instruments at a time: a large base drum, cymbals, a bagpipe, and other things too. Today, as I seek my goals, I see myself in a sense as following in the footsteps of that musi-

---

1 This article appeared a few days after Moreno's death in "The Public Education Monitor," published by the National Council of Education in December 1919. (Author unknown).

* Translator's Note: "Pancho" is a popular nickname for "Francisco" in Spanish-speaking countries.

cian. Sometimes I feel like I'm not playing all the instruments of my makeshift band very well, but then I just try harder." This statement indeed sums up Moreno's character. The endeavors of this one-man band, however, were crowned with the most brilliant success.

Moreno was a distinguished aristocrat. Three of his major accomplishments have become true chapters in the history of Argentina. First and foremost was his exploration –one might say discovery– of Patagonia. As if this feat were not formidable enough, his legacy includes the La Plata museum, and the defense of Argentine interests in the border dispute with Chile.

The museum and its collections are the products of Moreno's work. He did not want to simply warehouse or display a brief, lifeless exhibition. His purpose was to build a center to inspire a wide range of studies on a par with the Smithsonian Institute, and he achieved that goal.

What fair-minded Argentine could fail to recognize that Moreno alone asserted our sovereignty over thousands of leagues of land in Patagonia? Even the Chileans and the British arbiter recognized that fact.[2]

A work of such magnitude required extraordinary commitment and superhuman efforts. Moreno undertook that task with unwavering determination. The purity of his patriotic devotion, unparalleled among all but a handful of illustrious Argentine heroes, was the force that fueled his resolute action. Pancho Moreno was obsessed with a love of country, and that love is what fed his will power. Moreno's individualism, strange as it may seem, was selfless. His country is what gave meaning to his life. When opposing interests rallied against him, rather than respond with like bitterness, he would merely offer his favorite observation, "This will reas-

---

[2] Excerpt from the letter dated August 11, 1902, and written by the British arbiter, Sir Thomas Holdich, a colonel, to Moreno: "I have repeatedly stated that everything the Argentine government obtains west of the continental divide, it will owe exclusively to you."

sure you of the need to educate the people." Moreover, when others insisted that he publicly defend his own record, he invariably responded: "No, it could be detrimental to the work if my name were used as a banner. This is not about me. It is about the work." His patriotism was so lofty that he was a humanist and an Americanist as much as he was an Argentine.

Towards the end of his life, his greatest concern was his isolation and "being unable to serve." "I can't sleep," he wrote in October 1918, "thinking about what needs to be done to protect this country and make it even greater. I have so little strength, so few resources and so little time to get my message across to the people Buenos Aires, a place so foreign to the natives. I remember the past so vividly, and it is hard to come to the realization that my life is swiftly coming to an end. But isn't life without service harder still?"

Those heartbreaking days when Moreno was "unable to serve" were a bitter time for him. Inactive and poverty stricken, dark shadows overtook his imagination. He felt misunderstood and feared that his services would go unrecognized by the country. "There is so much I'd like to do," he wrote on one of many scraps of paper later found in his desk, "so much that needs to be done for my country! But how? I am 66 years old and don't have a cent. How important is money in such a case? I have given eighteen hundred leagues and a National Park for the benefit of future citizens, so that they may find solace and renewed strength to serve this country. Yet I have nothing to give my children, not even a tiny plot in which to bury my ashes. I was the one who staked a claim over eighteen hundred leagues of disputed territory for Argentina, when no one else could defend those lands and secure Argentine sovereignty over them. Still, there is no place to put my ashes, not even a 20 by 20 centimeter box. My ashes would take up so little space. Yet it they were spread out, they might stretch across all the land I acquired for my country. It would no doubt be a very thin layer but it would be visible to the eyes of those who are, in fact, grateful."

Pancho Moreno can rest assured that he has achieved immortality. There is a halo, an aura, shining over his work, and thus shining over him. Argentina will never forget her national hero, who did so much for the country's moral and material growth. History will note Moreno's great work and his accomplishments in obtaining knowledge about nature, so that man may better adapt to nature, as a condition for achieving life, progress and morality.

TO THE READER

In compiling my father's memoirs, written between 1906 and 1919, I have strived to leave his manuscripts unaltered. I have, however, chosen to omit some passages or documents altogether, since my father's restless pen often intermingled the tales of his travels with issues derived from his role as expert adviser for the Argentine government in delineating the border with Chile. For this reason, there are gaps in continuity. Many of the documents were misplaced at the time of my father's death. Yet I have been able to piece them together as a result of a patient search spanning more than twenty years. This compilation is now offered to the reader in hopes that it will spark an interest in the region my father loved so much.

This region includes the Nahuel Huapi National Park, and both Lanín and Los Alerces National Reserves. Today, thanks to a major government effort, this area has been transformed into an "international tourism center," just what my father envisaged when he made the donation in 1903 creating the initial core of Nahuel Huapi National Park. It was my father's prediction that "once this area becomes an inalienable part of the public domain, it will become a hub of great social and intellectual activities, and hence a magnificent resource for mankind."

Eduardo V. Moreno
Buenos Aires, 1942.

PART I

Overland crossing to Río Negro
First Visit to Nahuel Huapi
1875/1876

PREFACE REGARDING THE FIRST TRIP TO NAHUEL HUAPI

No sooner had I put together my Santa Cruz and Río Negro[1] collections than I headed for the province of Entre Rios. I wanted to compare, however tenuously, tertiary formations in Patagonia vis-à-vis those in Paraná. I traveled from Victoria to the ravines and obtained excellent soil samples from that part of our territory revealing the soil's past and present life forms. Later in Vitel, I collected additional materials and wrote about them in two short reports. One was published in the "Compte Rendu" of Stockholm's Prehistoric Anthropology and Archeology Conference (1874) and the other in the "Newsletter of the National Science Academy of Córdoba," whose founder, Doctor Burmeister, designated me as a corresponding member.

I continued my travels and reached the Blanca Grande Lake, west of Azul, in the province of Buenos Aires, where the great majority of the troops were camped along a line separating them from Indian country. I collected an abundant array of skeletons and skulls from the cemeteries of subjugated Indians living near the area surrounding Azul and Olavarría (See Appendix, First Letter).

In Blanca Grande for the first time, I heard the melancholy, "lights out," ordering those who guard the western plains, always armed and on the alert, to take a rest. I also heard the cheerful reveille. In that remote region, where only Indians dared to tread, chasing ostriches, herds of horses and cattle, or taking women captive, the trumpet call soothed cattle ranchers' fears of sudden Indian attacks. There I saw brave

IMPORTANT NOTE: Proper names or geographic locations may show misspellings and errors because they were taken from illegible documents or from Moreno's own typed manuscripts that he had not finished editing.

[1] Obtained while I participated, *ad honorem*, in the expedition to Santa Cruz on board "La Rosales," a sailing vessel belonging to the National Fleet.

military couriers who brought news from faraway forts despite the constant danger of being stabbed or having their throats slit. I remember the able-bodied soldiers, many of whom had been sentenced to serve in the army. They had a carefree attitude towards the perils and sacrifices demanded by their extremely hard lives. I can still see their smiling faces as they unsaddled their panting horses. Often a horse would collapse from exhaustion when freed from the bit and other riding gear. These soldiers were always on call, ready for action despite the many risks. It was encouraging to learn that in some areas of the United States, convicts sentenced to long years of hard labor are bound solely by their word of honor, that is to say that they promise to serve their time and they do. When our line soldiers serve under similar conditions, desertion is rare, even though it would be an understandable response to the unrelenting dangers of military service. They too have kept their word of honor.

How could I forget the prisoner who a short time later served me so well during my first trip to Nahuel Huapi? There was also another prisoner with Indian features named Chino Melgarejo, who was a messenger of Caudillo Lopez Jordán's army, later sent to the fifth regiment. I will always remember his loyalty during the hardships endured in 1880 when I was held captive and escaped from the Indian camps of Caleufú.

When will the book be written that records the story of a soldier,[2] as depicted by Blanes, the Uruguayan painter: the story of an impromptu fighter who, having lost his leg to a cannon ball during the first English Invasion, used a knife to cut off its dangling last remains, tied his threadbare shirt to the stomp and dragged himself back into line, weapon in hand, so as not to lose his place among the decimated ranks? Neither do we hear about the "doomed" soldier who fell

---

2 Similar anecdotes could be written about heroic sailors.

during the fratricidal "Revolución del Parque" and whose nose, mouth and tongue were shattered by machine gun fire. When asked what he was feeling, he responded by scribbling the words, "Nothing, but please place a wreath over my captain's body for me," as his captain lay dead by his side.

Those soldiers were remarkably loyal. It is fair to say that if they were fated for having done wrong in the past, they fully made up for their misdeeds later on by contributing an exceptional share of manliness, affection, and glory. When I look back on these veterans who would never make it through alive I am consumed with passion by this subject. They were "cannon fodder," dispensable human targets felled by their enemies' spears, lassoed stones (*boleadoras*), and long *facón* knives.

So attracted was I to the endless plains, the mystery of the West, that I made up my mind to penetrate deeper into these lands to study the area in the North of Patagonia being contested by Chile. Indeed, I had failed to gain access to that area by way of the Santa Cruz River. I reread the account of Cox's crossing of the Andes by way of Nahuel Huapi. He had tried to reach the Atlantic but had been unsuccessful, however, as opposition from east coast Indians forced him to return to Chile. In Río Negro I had heard about an easy pass across the Andean Cordillera almost level with the plain. It intrigued me that Cox's map showed a solid mountain chain in that place around Lake Lácar, while my sources, the Río Negro Indians, had assured me there was a mountain pass, free of snow in winter. I searched around for ways to manage the crossing from east to west, an even more intriguing feat given no one had ever been able to reach the lake from the Atlantic, not even the explorer Basilio Villarino. He had made it as far as the Collón-Curá River, a tributary of the Limay, and then had headed upstream for a certain distance. Major Bejarano would also visit that same spot in 1872. I presented the idea to the Argentine Scientific Society and it was accepted. With support from that organization and from the provincial government, I set out on my journey in September of 1875.[3]

It was my objective to travel by land to Patagones, thoroughly explore the Río Negro and Limay valleys, reach the Nahuel Huapi Lake and take one of the many mountain passes in the area to cross over to Chile. I had been assured it was a relatively easy task. In those days the railroad went only as far as Las Flores, two hundred kilometers from Buenos Aires. A message delivery service operated weekly to Azul and monthly to Bahía Blanca. This long stretch –one thousand kilometers– covered a practically uninhabited area, and it was not unusual for Indians to attack and plunder

[3] Since Moreno had informed General Bartolomé Mitre (whom he had always admired and appreciated) of his plans, Mitre, in a letter dated October 20, 1875, addressed to Diego Barros Arana in Chile, put in a good word for the young explorer. He writes, "...I almost forgot to mention another young naturalist for whom we have high hopes. He is still very young, but has already made a name for himself in Europe, due to a series of essays on prehistoric Patagonia published in the *Revue d'Anthropologie de Broca*. These articles are based on independent studies he conducted in the region. Another of his works dealt with the subject of early Indian artifacts from Buenos Aires province. It was published in the *Boletín de Ciencias Exactas* of the province of Córdoba. Both are completely original pieces of work and shed new light on the subject. His major work, however, is a Museum of Anthropology, Archeology and Paleontology set up in his own home, a collection he himself assembled which includes more than 400 skulls from different indigenous races. It is surely the most comprehensive American skull collection in existence. He is intelligent, educated, and has a vast library of books about the Americas. Above all, he is a passionate traveler and is courageous enough to confront any danger or hardship as he ventures into unknown regions. He has studied the geology of the area and has collected items revealing its natural history. His name is Francisco P. Moreno and he is now on his way to Chile. I highly recommend him to you and your friends.

The young Mr. Moreno will be making an exploratory voyage. He will traverse the Pampas and cross the Andes Range from Carmen de Patagones Fort, by way of Nahuel Huapi, roughly following Cox's itinerary, although in the opposite direction. He will then probably head towards Perú, in order to enrich and perfect his skull collection, and to complete or even correct in part the studies conducted by Tschudi and Morton.

I have before me the first letter he wrote about his trip and a rough sketch of his projected journey. He is presently exploring the Río Colorado and says that he expects to be in Chile between February and March."

messenger posts, leaving the locals' throats slashed. Today's inhabitants are unaware of the horrors endured in that place. They reap the benefits of golden harvests in this area, one of the first regions to earn the name "the breadbasket of the world."

It was undoubtedly not the most convenient time to travel. Rumor had it that bands of Indians from the region of Salinas Grandes in the province of Buenos Aires were on the offensive. We frequently got word of their border raids, a prelude to the major invasions yet to come. Nevertheless, I found myself increasingly drawn to Nahuel Huapi. It was the lure of the unknown even more than the beautiful lake that attracted my attention.

It never ceased to amaze me how a vigorous nation in possession of huge expanses of land stretching from the tropics to the Antarctic could be so indifferent to conducting a feasibility study for their use, especially when in doing so, the country's sovereignty could be asserted over territories that nature had so generously bestowed upon it. Our indifference towards what we claim to have inherited from Spain has led to the actual loss of sizable portions of that legacy. The wresting of what was ours without so much as consulting us was the product of our ignorance of its worth, for which not so much as a shred of justification has subsequently been found. Our comfortable enjoyment of material goods has caused us, on more than one occasion, to forget our duty to our country. We allow ourselves to be absorbed by a cosmopolitan lifestyle; then we take refuge in the fleeting memory of past glories as a way to hide our current weakness of character. Drowning in decadent luxury, we assume those accomplishments were achieved by people who bear no resemblance to us today. That being said, it seems as though

---

This letter was published on July 15, 1879 in the Review of Science, Arts, and Letters, Volume I, Number 5, under the heading "*A Letter about American Literature*".

we excuse ourselves for such weakness without stopping to think that all men are equal when they equally love the land on which they were born. Future generations will call for a rendering of accounts from our generation as to what Argentina once was but is no longer. Our statues and other honors will come down, because those enshrined thereby knowingly brought harm upon the country without reflecting even for a moment on the liability so incurred.

Why should we burden our descendants with such disgraceful lies as to our history? It is with that in mind that I have wanted to make my contribution by taking the desert and turning it into non-barren land. It is a fact that upon discovering its untapped riches we will become stronger and thus better able to defend it.

Young and enthusiastic, I was convinced that if we made way for civilization to reach the Andes, replacing lazy Indians with hardworking men throughout our fertile plains, forests and mountains, we would help mitigate some of the damage caused by this disastrous lack of foresight. I wanted to spread the word about my country's rich soil and I refused to be deterred by difficulties that others whom I was trying to emulate had been able to overcome. Indeed, they had pursued the same ideals determinedly and under circumstances thousands of times more adverse.

OVERLAND CROSSING TO RÍO NEGRO
FIRST VISIT TO NAHUEL HUAPI

At postal stations along the way, I received news of recent atrocities involving Indians who had burnt down homes. This was proof to me of the need to change the ways of the savages. Calderón, the postmaster, pointed out large columns of smoke in the distance that periodically signaled disasters occurring far on the horizon. He responded to my plans by saying, "Don't go, my friend, the Indians will kill you." Yet I was an idealistic 23-year-old; hardships and forewarnings merely reinforced my determination. Thus, I was undaunted by the scattered settlements adorned with gravesites, or by the armed inhabitants whose livestock grazed under vigilant eyes. I had to go on.

Bahía Blanca still looked as dull as I had left it two years before during my first visit to the future "Liverpool of the South" (Appendix, Second Letter). On my way from the port to the village I was lucky to escape from the Indians who two hours later tried to take the village by storm.

After a short excursion to Punta Alta, the site of the fossil deposits studied by Darwin in 1834, I set off on a cross country expedition from Bahía Blanca to Carmen de Patagones, (Appendix, Third Letter dated October 13, 1875), a dangerous route in general and all the more so in those days. Pichún, a tribal leader from the Indian camps at Salinas Grandes, who had a fierce reputation, roamed the trails, eager to pounce on herds of cattle in transit. I would have been ill advised to follow the usual path. Instead, I decided to travel across Indian Territory in a way that assured safe passage, by bowing to the barbarian authority.[1] We were so weak then!

---

[1] To the Bahía Blanca Military Commander: Whereas Francisco P. Moreno is traveling through Roma, Salinas Chicas, and Colorado to get to Río Negro and find medicinal herbs, therefore the Argentine Government hereby petitions the cacique General Manuel Namuncurá and all his Indian chiefs to refrain

After checking out the Punta Alta fossil deposits discovered by Darwin, I headed out with two young Indian men for Nueva Roma, the last military post on the frontier. It's a good thing we went in that direction and then through Salinas Chicas and Calaveras. For when we arrived a few days later at the Romero Grande sand dunes, an area notorious for frequent surprise Indian attacks, I noticed that Pichún had been there. Fresh spear tracks were still visible on the sand.

At the Colorado River we were met by a solemn reception from the Picunche chieftains: Queupumilla, Yancamilla, and Guenupilla, on behalf of Commanding Officer Bernal, who was in charge of that frontier zone, (Appendix, Part I, Letters 4, 5, and 6). Then I made my way to the Río Negro, ready to face the rough road to Chile. Not a soul was in sight except for a few miserable forts dotting the empty landscape alongside the river in Mercedes, and Outposts 1 and 2. They amounted to mere hellholes where our young officers and soldiers risked their lives every day. They endured rugged conditions and deprivation in order to fulfill their duty to their country. Despite the dangers they faced owing to government neglect, they did not complain.

Before me lay salt deposits, sand dunes, and thorny bushes, giving the panorama an arid look, yet the future of those lands was bright. Part of it was already crossed by railroad almost to Carmen de Patagones. This wilderness area was owned by the province of Buenos Aires, which had conducted a thorough topographical study that I had the good fortune of directing. It laid the groundwork for the use of water from the Río Colorado and the Río Negro for purposes of irrigation. It would thus become possible to plant vineyards and other crops in this vast territory, on a scale as large as or even larger than that of Mendoza and San Juan provinces. Perhaps

---

from blocking his way or from harming him. —Daniel Cerri, Bahía Blanca, October 7, 1875.

agriculture would be even more successful here, given the proximity to the best seaports and rivers, one of which was navigable. I wish that area had a school where people could learn to take advantage of local resources. Perhaps it could be placed at the site where in times past the robust carob tree grew. In those unhurried times it was known as the "Walichu" tree. I remember seeing it adorned from head to foot with colorful scraps of ponchos and other objects that hung from its branches. These offerings were made to F'Ta-Huentrú, the "Great Man," the embodiment of the concept of one who dispenses good and evil. Through such offerings, the native tribes prayed for help on their marches, whether in peace or in war.

Agriculture and cattle-raising now enjoy prosperity here, and the prospects for better transportation facilities are encouraging. Already, new villages have replaced rundown forts and the transformation is obvious. When I thought about the area's utter desolation and all the difficulties I had once encountered there, I could not help but feel a sense of satisfaction. Railroads and cars had taken the place of plunderers and mayhem. I wondered what had become of the clustered crosses I had often found along the way. I could still remember the bloodstained clothes of troopers whom the fearsome Pichún had slaughtered a few days after I passed through Romero Grande, a horrific sight I encountered months later on my way back from Lake Nahuel Huapi. It pleased me immensely, however, to think about the changes that would be brought about by rational land development and the ripple effect they would have along the coastline once the need for port facilities could no longer be ignored.

In the old days while traveling on the Río Negro by steamship or sailboat, I was told that access to that river would be most difficult if not impossible for ships of large tonnage. The Bay of San Blas, however, reportedly had the potential to become a viable shipping port for transporting the products of the vast area bordering the river. I set out to confirm this theory by visiting the surrounding area while I collected items for my museum. I realized the future held great promise for this region. As I saw it, building dikes would transform these flooded lowlands. My findings would prove useful to science thirty years later. My quest had proved fruitful as well. Local cemeteries yielded the remains of former inhabitants whose workmanship was reflected in several stone implements. I added them to my collection.

Not without difficulty, I managed to find an experienced Indian guide to take me to the camp of Chief Shaihueque, lord of the crossing between Argentina and Chile. As it happens, my only guide at this crucial juncture was a prisoner on loan from a garrison whose commander also ran the penitentiary. We first re-examined the lodgings of former indigenous tribes and their burial grounds, while we developed better relations with the Tehuelche, Gennaken and Mapuche tribes.

We set off towards the end of November, heading west along the voluminous river. Four Indian guides drove our horses and the fifty mares that would serve as our main food source. We began our long marches through the silent valley. The only sounds were the cry of the teru-teros (long-legged plover), the murmuring of the Pampero wind shaking the white plumes of the Paja Brava and rustling the willows' drooping branches, and the wide river rushing over trees uprooted in former floods.

Every now and then, bands of friendly Indians pierced the silence and cheered us up. About a hundred of them traveled with us to Chichinal, now called General Roca, (Appendix, Part I, Letters 7 and 8). They made the days go by faster as they enthusiastically hunted ostriches. A few days into the hunt, their lookouts spotted the Picunches, their sworn enemies, who were making their way to Chile with a herd of cattle they had stolen in Romero Grande after killing the herders. As I previously mentioned, this incident happened three days after I passed through those feared sand dunes.

In Chichinal we saw the dust kicked up by the missing herd. Eager to feast on the animals, our companions set out to catch their prey. Practically naked, and just carrying their spears, rock-studded lassos known as *"bolas,"* and sharp knives, they clung to their fighting-horses as they crossed the river. We kept pressing west, my Indian helpers driving the mares. Amid shouts of "giddy up" and "mare", I dreamt of the future of this land whose dust was choking me.

During those hunts with elusive nomadic tribes, or when we'd take a moment to rest, I would often talk to my Indian guides about the future of these territories without stopping to think whether in my need to find an outlet for my aspirations I was exposing myself to harm. I would speak to them as I satiated my hunger with raw intestines from a worn-out mare or eagerly watched a tasty skewered ostrich being barbecued over heated rocks, a cooking method that preceded the use of pottery. It gave me great pleasure to recall this scenario twenty-five years later when I revisited the same locales and saw that they had blossomed into towns. Perhaps my former listeners' grandchildren were attending the local schools.

We crossed the Limay River where it meets the Neuquén, and both rivers merge into the Río Negro. This place, now known as Confluencia, is not far from the capital of the province of Neuquén. Our crossing made use of the most primitive methods. Four dry willow branches served as an excellent luggage raft. We swam across while clinging to our horses' manes as we braved the swift current. From there we proceeded for a long stretch along the wide "Chilean Trail," also known as "Robbers' Lane." This trail was blazed by hundreds of thousands of cows that the Indians stole from the Argentine Pampas. The herds would then be acquired by wealthy Chilean ranchers in a series of barter transactions, and fattened for market on Chile's large alfalfa plantations.

The Limay whimsically meanders through the center of the valley, skirting the steep red canyons. As we hiked through one of them, crossing the hills of Chocón-Geyú, we came across the vestiges of a tragic event. Nine burial mounds made of loose stones and dry branches covered the skeletal remains of an entire Indian family. According to my companions, one winter, these hapless travelers had come across the Picunches, who had taken off with their horses. Huddled together in freezing temperatures they had died of exposure under a blanket of snow, unable to reach the willows in plain sight at the foot of the deep ravine. In the aftermath of their death, each Indian passer-by would add a rock to those initially placed when the bodies were found. As time went by and the sense of devotion waned, travelers would merely show their respects with a small branch. Later, branches gave way to a shred of poncho or a strip of the blanket trousers known as *chiripás*. We ourselves laid one such piece of cloth over the tomb.

Such was the story told to me by my Indian companions. Were their tales of woe true or unverified supposition handed down from past generations? I do not know. What I do know is that many now extinct early tribes had the custom of building similar burial mounds in the highlands south of the Río Negro. I have observed such gravesites in some of the Northern provinces and it is still quite common for similar tomb markers to be placed over the dead where an underground burial is not feasible. When traveling through the northwestern highland mesas along Andean paths that connect La Rioja, Catamarca, and Salta to Copiapó and Atacama, I have seen cairns covering whitened heaps of bones. These are the remnants of unfortunate travelers caught in a sudden snowstorm in this vast desolate expanse.

We saw the plunging canyons of the Chocón-Geyú. Villarino, the explorer, said they looked like ruins of buildings. On a clear night, it appears as if a city with spectacular domes and formidable towers has been carved out of red rock. We crossed Cumlelfen (the "Pink Pampa"), past Picunleufú (River of the Picunches, or "the People of the North"), and came across the first apple trees, which gave the region its name: "Manzana-Geyú." We did not hear the firing of shotguns, undoubtedly because it was summer. According to the Indians, you can hear them in the wintertime at Huinca-Tralcan-Geyú ("The Land of the Christians' Thunder").

We left the Limay at Ranquelloao, making our way through basalt canyons and then through the granite rock sierras of Persquin-puramue and Collón-Curá, which lead to the river of the same name. In Neumucó ("Stinking Waters"), we ran into the first Indians. They were quite stunned, as our arrival had been predicted in Chief Shaihueque's "dreams," (a "dream" that followed the arrival of a messenger sent by the "friendly" Indians of the Río Negro, as I found out later).

The troubling news was that the natives were up in arms because of delays in the delivery of food rations that the government had agreed to distribute. Their discontent was further incited by Chief Manuel Namuncurá from "Salinas Grandes." His goal was to swell up his ranks by winning them over. United they would stop the government from the further incursion of the boundary line being planned by the Minister of War, Adolfo Alsina.

This state of affairs cast a chill over our own prospects. Our expedition had reached the same spot that Villarino, the explorer, traversed almost one hundred years earlier when he carried out his memorable explorations on the banks of the Collón Curá ("Stone Mask"). At this point we were forced to await the messenger sent to inform Shaihueque of my arrival. He was to relate to him my desire to greet him in his tent, an indispensable formality that would prevent serious trouble later. My objective was not only to study the regions along the way and cross the Cordillera to Chile, but also to see the Indians in their surroundings, far from civilization, by living in an Indian hut. I wanted to gather information from among these tribes facing extinction. I wanted to document what I simply knew from hearsay since that method fell short of my goals.

I do not intend this piece of writing to be a complete account of my journey. I would just like to show how my plan evolved. I have omitted certain events that might well enliven the story but would make it too long. Though at this moment I must hold back in recounting these events, it is not without a sense of nostalgia, for the years have a way of making the memories tender and sweet, even if they were bitter at the time. I hope I will have enough time to report on my impressions of the primitive environment in which these native tribes lived. Indeed, I was the last one to experience them before they were wiped out by those who never bothered to listen to opposing views. I lived among these self-reliant natives, masters of highlands and plains, followers of no laws other than those imposed by their limited needs. They fed off "the animals of their lands," wore the clothes made by their women, and waged war from time to time as a way to deal with issues of witchcraft or after drinking binges.

The time I spent in the remote tents of Caleufú facing the Andes range is hard to forget. I remember the solemn silence of the Indians, whose intentions were unknown to me when I arrived. I remember the sad, monotonous chanting alternating with the cry of the women who completed the warriors' circle. Later I learned that their laments expressed warm feelings for the Christian traveler, who had suffered on his long journey from the sea ("The Great Lake"). I remember the chief and the able-bodied young men acting high and mighty as they took in the fact that their name was actually known in faraway lands. There was a series of never-ending talks with the chief inside his big tent to obtain permission for our passage to Chile. His behind-the-scenes-advisers, the Chilean mestizos, as well as Loncochino, secretary of the "Supreme Government of Las Manzanas," as it was called, and Valdés, the chieftain's silversmith, persuaded him that it was dangerous for the Mapuches to reveal the location of Andean passes to Argentines, as there was talk of expanding the frontier. Of course, the Chileans were planning to do the exact same thing at the time with their own frontiers. Once they had found the passes, it would be easy to reach the Indian encampments and annihilate the inhabitants. Moreover, the Indians would not be able to prevent the slaughter. They were up against the new Remington rifle, used in the Revolution of 1874 in which Catriel's tribes participated. The weapon was already known to them, as news of its terrifying destruction had reached Las Manzanas.

I could fill up many pages with stories about the war council held on the plains of Quem-Quen-Treu following these meetings. However, this "Aucatrahum" was not the only time I was to meet with the Mapuche chieftains, so I will refer my readers to accounts of my 1880 predicament, narrated further ahead in these pages. Suffice it to say that 453 Indians armed with spears attended the council, in which I explained the objectives of my visit to the main chieftains, convened by Shaihueque, Ñancucheo, Molfinqueupu, Naquipichuin and Jankakirque. This "parliament" met for five hours, on horseback, as the chieftains, following the advice of tribal elders, backed Shaihueque's refusal to let us through. They not only opposed our passage to Chile but also reneged on the promise they had previously granted to allow passage from Caleufú to Mendoza. I was told to go back the same way I had come, and to consider myself lucky that I was being allowed to do so.

A major Indian revolt was brewing in reaction to the delay in the delivery of government food rations. Namuncurá was enticing the natives with his repeated calls to arms. While I was there, I read his inflammatory remarks. He urged the Indians to invade Buenos Aires en masse to ensure success in numbers. His letters were not accepted by the Mapuche chiefs, who were eager to remain on friendly terms with the Argentine government. Still, my presence annoyed the chieftains. It had a negative impact on their plans, already underway, which called for some groups to heed the Ranquel chief's instigations. This tribal chief appealed to the easygoing youths by showering them with gifts of valuable silver garments and captive women. He led them to believe they could obtain similar riches in the looting to come.

The so-called parliament held on the Collón-Curá flatlands was vividly reminiscent of similar councils described by the Chilean author Ercilla. The oratory of the elders had the same flavor as those of Araucanian chieftains of Ercilla's era. Occasionally, they would carry me back to those days, as I tried to fill in my interpreter's incomplete translations with memories of the sixteenth-century epic in honor of the Araucanians. I can still hear the paused but resounding, brittle ringing of bells from Molfinqueupú bringing back memories of centuries-old struggles between the Indians, who owned the land, and the Spaniards who strove to take it away. I see before me the old, handsome figure of the Indian chief, his weathered skin the color of mature oak, his rough white hair decorated with black eagle feathers, a wide headband across his forehead.

From my standpoint, I could clearly see Lake Lácar basin and the green patches of grass dotting the fertile plains of Chapelcó, where years later, Fort Maipú and then Fort San Martín de los Andes would be erected. This was the site of one of the Chilean passes of which the natives had informed me. The source of a river that ran across the mountains towards the west was also found there.

Later, I spent wonderful days at the Indian camps of Ñancucheo, by the Chimehuin River, across from the extinct Lanín Volcano. The volcano is covered with snow more than halfway down its slopes. The snow is interspersed with groves of tall majestic Pehuenes (Araucaria imbricata), and surrounded by sweeping grassy meadows.

Living at camp I had the rare opportunity to witness an initiation ritual rarely seen by a traveler in that primitive environment: the "huecururá," which celebrates a young Mapuche girl's readiness for marriage. There I saw the last wooden mask ever used in indigenous festivities in that region. It was an ethnographic artifact of the utmost significance, as it provided evidence of the exceptionally vast area in which masks have been used. It spans the American continent from Alaska to Patagonia.[2]

---

[2] Tierra del Fuego tribes use a similar object for their humble celebrations: a red and white striped bonnet with holes for the eyes and made of bark from an Antarctic beech tree. It replaces the mask most probably used by their

Travelers who have visited the southern tribes of the Americas cannot help but note the visible ethnic similarities that exist among some tribes today, even though they inhabit regions at a far distance from one another. The old Mapuche chiefs, for instance, remind me of pictures I have seen of Native American chiefs in the Western United States. Their customs were analogous. The discovery of the mask at the Ñancucheo tent and its use in the "huecucurá" ceremony, no doubt an ancient one in which the medicine man takes part, point to similar rituals carried out in Northern regions. This may amount to further evidence of more or less direct contact among American groups of the past, and of ethnic relationships among groups separated by great distances. The topic is an interesting one, but must also be left for another occasion.

When we speak of American Man, or European Man, Asian Man, African Man, etc., we are merely making broad, conventional generalizations. It would be difficult to establish any type of kinship between the Tehuelches of Magellan's days and some of the races whose remains were left behind in the Río Negro valley, or between Eskimos and Aleuts. Indeed, such a task would be just as difficult as to establish a connection between the people who left us the dolmen funeral monuments and those of the funeral mounds of Northern Europe, between the Samoyeds and the Veddas, or any other group, for that matter.

I felt content along the banks of the Malleco, its crystal-clear waters jet-black as they mirrored the ebony-colored basalt columns of Pungechaf, and further along, at the breathtaking meadows of wild strawberry fields, in a place called "Quellén-Geyú" or "Quillén-Hos." This meadow is crossed by a creek whose waters irrigate a pristine valley of

---

ancestors from warmer regions. Olden day Peruvians placed silver masks over some of their dead, and some stone masks have been found in the northwestern Calchaquí valleys. They are now housed at the La Plata Museum.

the same name. I reveled in the natural beauty of this land of promise. What a positive transformation it would undergo once festivals exulting labor replaced the orgies with which the Indians celebrated the unrestrained flow of liquor from Valdivia across the mountain passes!

Against this backdrop, my work was progressing well. The collections in my museum would represent the soil of a truly privileged region. As I looked across the horizon, I could see the outlines of a landscape yet unknown on the map of Argentina. Yet I had such great expectations for my country that complete satisfaction eluded me. I pondered those lands yet unknown to civilization, and my heart sank as I considered how much these territories were neglected by those who had the capacity to incorporate them. Pessimist that I am when it comes to government policies, I imagined that soon this land would be worked by "pioneers," Argentine born or nationalized. My pessimism has borne out. It has been thirty-four years since Chief Ñancucheo lost his life defending the soil on which he was born, thirty-four years since a strong and useful race was destroyed by violent, unnecessary means. Today flourishing towns are found in the region, part of which is crossed by rail. Yet the region's progress is hindered on account of grants awarded time and again to stock market barons each time the frontier expanded. As a result, dozens of leagues are in the hands of a lucky few who do nothing to increase their value. "What use is this land?" I have heard this said by quite a few of those who held the fortune and even the fate of the country in their hands.

If you, the reader, were to look at a map of the area, you would be astonished to find that a large portion of the eastern and northern sections of Nahuel Huapi, this beautiful piece of Argentine "Switzerland," belongs to a very small number of owners. Most of them bought it dirt-cheap as a special favor from friends in government. A closer look would reveal that deeds were recently executed in such a manner that owners have seen the size of their plots increase one hundred fold. The maps showing the location of these land grants are perhaps less accurate than those of lunar colonies described in some science fiction novels. However, it doesn't take much to know that it is in the national interest to study and utilize every corner of this vast triangle wedged between the Limay and Neuquén Rivers and the Andes mountains.

Sadly, the average Argentine of today takes more interest in personal animosities and ambitions than in learning about the lands where this heroic struggle is taking place. Before he realizes it, someone in the know has surreptitiously pulled another strip of land from the public domain, yet nobody notices and nobody cares. An official study, conducted over the last two years, regarding the region located between the Atlantic coast and the Andes, in the area influenced by the railroad at Port San Antonio going down to Lake Nahuel Huapi, has been developed into a magnificent book. This book sheds light on the vast natural resources encountered in the Andes region.[3]

As I was talking to myself under the shade of the apple trees, two Indian travelers approached intending to cross the river. They were traveling from Salinas Grandes to Villa Rica, Chile. They informed me of Chief Catriel's revolt and the Indian raids with their trail of murder and plunder. What made the situation worse was the immediate threat of a new, more massive rebellion to be carried out by the Andean tribes led by chief Reuquecurá.

I decided to hurry back to Buenos Aires in order to warn frontier communities so I beat a hasty retreat to Shaihueque's camp. Then I ventured out across the valley where Junín de los Andes stands today, making my way back to Caleufú. I traversed the high ridges that frame the majestic Lanín Volcano, an imposing presence my companions called

---

[3] I am writing this in March 1916. Note: The book referred to is entitled *El Norte de la Patagonia* ("The North of Patagonia") Hydrological Studies Commission; Bailey Willis, director, published by the Office of the Secretary of Public Works.

Quetropillán, and crossed other jagged Andean mountains beyond, green at the foothills, bluish in the middle and covered with immaculate snow at the summit. Dark gorges, deep gaps in that colossal geologic wall, gave evidence that there were many other passageways to Chile. These would be easy paths, without steep slopes to climb. They would not be unlike the ones found further to the north, shaded by Pehuén and Coihue trees, or by the apple trees that sprouted over the centuries from seeds cast out by the Indians on their way back over the mountains. They were returning home to freedom after being converted to Christianity in the faraway Jesuit missions to the west. The apple trees were also the only remnants of the expansion of Christianity in those remote territories. In their shadow, I have often stopped to remember the Christian martyrs who were sacrificed in such places.

It would have been easy for me to elude the watchful eye of my indigenous companions and make it across the mountains, thus fulfilling my desire to reach the Pacific by way of the Huahun path they continually followed. However, such behavior on my part would probably have renewed their suspicions of Argentine intentions and promises. They would have embraced Namuncurá's plan, taken the frontier communities by storm and plundered the area between Bahía Blanca and Azul. My limited personal satisfaction would have unleashed much bloodshed. Therefore, I settled for picturing those alluring passes in my mind, as I listened to my Indian helpers describe their forests and intricately tangled creeping vines.

I could have made it to Maiué, on the other side, in one day, across the passes made by the Huahun river, the outlet of Lake Lácar. Contrary to what Cox's map showed, the eastern banks of the lake were not flanked by mountains. Instead, one could clearly make out a vast plain. This indicated that the Andes were to the west not the east of the lake whose waters cut across the mountains and then emptied into the Pacific. I relinquished my initial yearning and headed up and down the plateaus, taking note of glacial phenomena represented by erratic fragments. Then I returned to the main Indian camp.

Our arrival at the Indian camp was well timed. While in the mesas, my traveling companions were fortunate enough to kill some ostriches along the way with their *bolas*, even though animal prey was scarce. The fresh meat came at a time when it was sorely needed in the camp. Caleufú was holding a celebration to receive the visit of the Cacique Quinchauala. Cacique Quinchauala was a good-natured Indian, to whom I am greatly indebted for having helped me obtain the permission I sought to travel to Nahuel Huapi. I was initially forbidden from going on account of a series of inexplicable events: Horses had collapsed; sickness spread; and thefts had increased as compared to the time prior to my arrival. Andean storms made their way down to the valley; fog engulfed the mesas, swallowing up the ostriches and guanacos. My few mares, once mine but "now Shaihueque's," were the only food in the camp. All this cast a shadow of doubt on the Christian, whose presence was blamed for these collective misfortunes of the Mapuches. I had to do a lot of persuading that day and I am grateful for my gift of elocution. With Quinchahuala's help I obtained permission to go to the lake.

Quinchahuala took a liking to me since I accepted a plate of food from him consisting of cornmeal with blood and raw tripe, and I ate it without a visible display of revulsion. That was proof of my outpouring friendship. Four years later, I found myself at that same place trying to get my hands on a piece of tripe or a blood-dripping bit of liver from a worn-out mare. These foods were eaten as a matter of course in the wilderness. Suffice it to say, the stomach adapts to the circumstances far beyond one's expectations.

I got Shaihueque to grant us a one-week absence, but to ensure our prompt return, he handpicked a horse for me to ride and gave us only one lamb for consumption. The picturesque trail that leads from Caleufú to the great lake, part of which stretched across the highlands, would later come to mind in the Vosges. Through rough, steep mountain slopes ran the Limay River in the middle of a deep gorge. My companions and I made our way under the shade of cypresses lining the steep edges of cliffs that plunged into the dark, rocky recesses of the wilderness, which were as awe-inspiring as the Black Forest. Water streaming down the cliffs mirrored distant forests that looked like man-made parks. There, I saw the rapids that witnessed Cox's shipwreck. Then I crossed the swift, deep currents of the awesome Traful, with its twists and bends as full of enchantment as they are with salmon and trout. The immense beauty of this region will come to be appreciated once we end our love affair with foreign lands and actually start to look at the wonders in our midst.

The splendor of these natural treasures became even more extraordinary as we advanced towards the south. Serenely beautiful vistas awaited us near an Argentine lake even more impressive than Geneva's Lake of Leman. When I finally got to the lake, I flew the Argentine flag. For the first time, our national colors, sky blue and white, were reflected in its fresh, crystal-clear waters. I drank profusely from these waters, the source of the Limay River. Between sips, I let my mind wander up the twists and turns of the Río Negro, from the Atlantic coast to the strawberry fields, peacefully reliving my trip from prehistoric mountain glaciers to the lakeshore. (January 22, 1876). Feeling quite pleased with myself, I thought about how easy it had been to reach my goal, and how I had persevered until obstacles had dissipated. I asked myself if those hardships had been less real than apparent. Hardly!

My spirit was as unruffled as the blue lake on that day, no trace of past storms. The effort exerted paled in comparison to the accomplishment: becoming the first white man to have made it to this place by way of the Atlantic. I had pinned my hopes on visiting Nahuel Huapi. Unfortunately, I did not get a chance to uncover its secrets, enter neighboring forests or reach the snow-capped peaks to the west. I did not have permission to go on, not even a few hours' walk from there to a pretty little place called Rinconada de Tequel Malal, where Cacique Inacayal lived. He would have given me a nice welcome. However, since we had to obey the strict orders imposed by the all-powerful Shaihueque, I set up camp under some tall cypress trees. I rested for two days, away from the Indians, dreaming about the future of this area, still unknown to the civilized people of my beloved country.

On the third day, I returned to Caleufú. By then I had grand ideas for the broad basin that stretched before my eyes to the southwest and reminded me of the Bariloche Pass. I said my good-byes to the lake until some later time when I could return. The sky cleared and I was able to see the white peak of Tronador Mountain. Southeast of the lake lay a plain with patches of yellow and green. Part of it looked like farmland. Thin clouds of smoke coming from the neighboring forest were the punctuation marks of a village. Perhaps it was the Valdiviano Indians who tilled the land. According to information I received from Río Negro, they grew barley and corn for Inacayal, who claimed ownership of the lakeshore. Unlike others, this Huiliche cacique, who later became my friend, embraced the trappings of civilization.

RETURN TO BUENOS AIRES
THE MARCH 1876 INVASION

B ack in Caleufú, I made renewed attempts to reach the beautiful Chilchiuma Range farther west. My Indian companions interpreted this *quechua* word as "dripping water." The Aimará name for the range has the same meaning,[4] which goes to show just how far-reaching the civilizing influence of Northern tribes was back then. Implements made by the Calchaquí Indians of Argentina's northwest were found as far south as Chubut by La Plata Museum employees.

In the foothills of this range lay the camp of Chief Chacayal, an enemy of the Christians. Cacique Shaihueque prudently forbade us to go near that camp. Since Chacayal was not trustworthy, and was prone to make things unpleasant for me, I thought it best to return immediately to Buenos Aires. I was prepared to go before the national government to defend the rights of the natives of these lands who had been "placed there by God."

Before I move on I would like to reminisce about two or three events I witnessed at the Indian camps. The first one took place around a large bolder, a protective stone. It was the chief's "totem," a ceremony designed to appease the gods, presided over by the tribe's medicine man. It involved the offering of Chilean peas and the juice of a tropical vine called *zarzaparrilla*, which when fermented is transformed into an infamous brew called *"queneupulcú."* I still get nauseated thinking about it. At the end of the ceremony, Chacayal gave us a sample of his oratory that lived up to his well-earned reputation as an orator in the camps.

It was the season for Mapuche festivals and celebrations.

---

4 It is not uncommon to find that in Patagonia, place names have the same meaning in Quechua as in Aimará (both Indian languages originated in Peru and Bolivia.)

One day we set out towards the hill, located on the banks of the Ya-Laley-Curá, where the large conglomerate mass of rock, now used as sacred stone, had fallen. This stone had been sent by God, according to the Machi, or medicine man. Its fall, he said, was meant as a warning from the Eternal Spirit, who was disappointed with the chief. Indeed, the chief had failed to give thanks to "F'ta Huentrú ("The Great Man") for his successful hunting expedition to Choele-Choel Island, which had experienced "few unpleasant moments." Presumably, the chief was aided by brightly shining stars and meteorites that carved a trail of light in the heavens. The presence of certain winds that, Indian legend has it, blow when a big chief embarks on a crusade, also worked in his favor. Yet Shaihueque had sacrificed neither animals nor liquor, a sacred ritual shared by all nations during their infancy. Oddly enough, the same bright light that guided the Three Magi on their way to Bethlehem was now lighting the way for the savage in the Pampa wilderness and guiding him in his depredations.

Warned by the purveyors of liquor that my mission at the Indian camp was far from peaceful, the old chief, who was already concerned about my presence there, decided to take advantage of the solemn moment and formal setting to voice his fears in the following terms:

"God meant for us to be born on these lands and they are ours. White men were born on the other side of the Big Waters. Later, they came to these lands even though the lands weren't theirs. They came to steal our animals and search for silver in the mountains. Our parents told us about this. They warned us never to forget that the Christians are the ones who are thieves, not us. Instead of asking for permission to live on our land, the Christians throw us out, so we defend ourselves. It may be true that they give us rations, but their rations are small payment for all that is being taken away from us. Now they don't even want to give us the rations. As wild animals become scarce, we are expected to starve to death. Tribes people have been too patient and Christians too proud. We are the legitimate landowners and they are the intruders. It is true that we promised

we would be friendly and not steal, but it was on condition that we are treated as brothers. As everyone knows, one year went by, then two years, then three years, and it has now been almost twenty years since we last made an invasion. We keep our promises. Christians have seen the "chilcas" (letters) sent to us by the Ranqueles (people from the plains where the "Paja Totora Ranquel" grass grows in the wetlands) and the Mamuelches (people from the Calden tree forests) asking us to join them in their raids. They know we have not agreed to do so. It's time they stopped making fools of us. All their promises are lies. Our friends and our captains, murdered by the Huincas (Christians), lie in sun-bleached bone heaps along the trail to Choele-Choel. They demand vengeance. We refuse to bury them because we want to be reminded of their presence so we never forget the soldiers' duplicity.

It's been a long time since their blood last stained my hands. I haven't eaten "caritún de huinca" (white man's flesh) since San Antonio, and I'm getting the urge.[5]

The Aucache says that the white man is coming to fight with us, now that they've stopped giving us rations. We don't say anything when they fight in Salinas, because Namuncurá is an intruder and God didn't give him that land. But we must fight for what God gave us. Quilapán fought in Chile, but Quilapán died. Now they are trying to wrest our land from us again, so they're looking for pathways to use to sneak up on us. The Christian has wrongfully deceived us by saying that he is a friend of our Patagones brothers. He has not been seen by Puelches, Moluches, Picunches, or Huiliches. He is

---

5 "Caritún means raw meat or flesh. It is an Indian expression used when Christians have been killed. It may be vaguely reminiscent of a distant past in which the Indians practiced cannibalism. In some instances, the Indians, their heads spinning after a killing spree, have drunk blood and eaten the heart of their white enemy. Chacayal is making reference to "San Antonio," an estancia in the south of Buenos Aires (San Antonio de Iraola), where, in 1855, a horrifying slaughter of Argentine soldiers and gauchos took place. Both Chacayal and Shaihueque took part in that raid. They described to me some of the most gruesome scenes. Only one soldier survived, who is presently employed as a guard at the National History Museum (1915).

Chilean; his blood will gush forth from his face, and his small heart will burst open when he confesses that he has deceived us."

Shaihueque managed to calm down his father-in-law and his captains. Only Yankakirque, known as "The Chief with Nine Women," who described himself as having a heart as big as his huge belly, remained unconvinced. He demanded proof of my sincerity in the form of a test of my physical strength. He vigorously squeezed my hand and tried to knock me off my horse. I bravely withstood the fierce pushing and shoving. Then we galloped full speed ahead, amid streams that cut across the thick underbrush and large rock formations, until we arrived at the second locale. There, the great invocation for the New Year was in full swing. It involved pleading for safe passage to Patagones.

My arrival provided an excellent excuse to extend the orgy. A new shipment of the infamous *aguardiente* liquor from Valdivia had just arrived and big leather pouches were full of fermented *zarzaparilla*.

In the grassy environs of the Indian camps of Caleufú, the old women had used branches to build big huts in an open circle that faced the rising sun. Hundreds of men, women, and children had gathered there to celebrate the omnipotence of F'ta Huentrú. Those who had come from far-away ranches used green branches to build small shelters. The shiny spearheads of the warriors, adorned with red feathers that glowed in the sun, were placed in front of the huts and makeshift shelters. The young women prepared *"caritún"* for the men's breakfast; the old women collected blood, gushing from the slaughtered mares' chests, and put it in wooden or silver vessels for the brave souls to savor before the ceremony started. Shaihueque, his family, and the Indian chiefs who were their guests were gathered in the big hut to celebrate for three days. The hut was built of the finest and richest woven fabrics. It was supported by forty huge spears painted red and decorated with feathers and pennants. The Argentine flag that I had brought with me, now unfurled and on prominent display, dominated the whole picture.

The young girls were clad in their best garments, their painted faces flush with red, blue, black, and white. They were cheerfully milling about. Their lips were exceptionally red, due to the application of a certain ointment made of bone marrow from a guanaco and colored with ochre used for protection against the dry mountain air. The young men wrapped themselves in luxury. They showed off their abundant silver, which exceeded iron by far. The lovesick resorted to everything in their power to please their "macoños," ("lovey doves" in the language of these indigenous people). One of them, a high-spirited fellow called Paishi, who perhaps had a rival, slathered his thick, black hair with the contents of an entire bottle of oil stolen from my helper, which dripped all over his face.

Shaihueque outdid them all in extravagance. Fully clad in the rubber suit I had given him as a token of my friendship, he glistened in the sun. His beautiful daughter Liquechen, who gave solace to the traveler in moments of illness, was enveloped in a white linen sheet. She had placed a mirror on her head for decoration. Her face was adorned with dots, made of little round stickers from the spools of thread I had given them, marked with the words "D.C. Thompson, No. 36." The two of them stood out in the crowd, together with an Indian fellow who wore a large woman's hat. The hat did not match his *quillango* fur blanket painted in garish colors. The red umbrella, unfurled in front of Ñancucheuque's tent, grabbed everybody's attention.

The fiesta started with a quest for the *Walichú*, or mean spirit. At the head of the hunting party were Umautesh, Shaihueque's second daughter, and Tacuman, his third son, who were both still very young. Umautesh rode a white horse painted with blue stripes, and her brother a bay horse painted with white stripes. Both animals were adorned with tiny bells and feathers. All day we gave chase to the *Walichú*, thrusting out our spears at him, stabbing at the air with increasing force in an effort to scare him away. Then we beat on the huts with sticks in case he might be hiding inside.

Once we were satisfied that he had been driven away, preparations for the dance began.

After building big bonfires and lining up the spears in two perfect rows in front of Lonco's (head-leader) *"ruca"* (hut), the dancing began. The young women took their place on one side and the men on the other. Marching and turning their heads sideways, they sang a monotonous tune to the music of the *"trutrucas."*[6] Some Indians used small flutes, made with tender cane branches, which merely whistled. Everything was accompanied by my helper's guitar.

The dance was a series of twists, turns, and bounces. The dancers formed two straight lines. Each dancer turned pirouettes, hopping along on one foot, then the other. The man's right foot was always opposite the woman's left foot or vice versa. The two sexes were separated by the rows of spears. At times all the men held onto one another's belts and all the women held onto one another's blankets. These women, especially the prettiest and fattest, who were the most attractive to the men, (for Patagonian Indians, fat is beautiful,) carried small sticks to hit their suitors when they reached the end of the line of spears. The sticks constituted their only defense in moments like these, as their fathers and brothers, if present, would do little to protect them against improprieties. Instead, they would laugh when the male dancers made passes at them. To my surprise, I saw that some of the female dancers had fake braids that they sometimes lost in the shuffle.

There was a certain magic to the setting. The monotonous music was accompanied by the old women's chanting, some-

---

[6] This instrument is made from the long, hollow cane of a *coligüé* vine, wrapped in tripe and having a bull's horn on its head. It is carried by two Indians. One is a musician who blows with all his might, only to produce dry and unpleasant sounds. The other carries the instrument on his shoulders. This instrument is in widespread use over great expanses by many indigenous South American tribes. Its sound reminds me of the "Alp horn," to which I awoke in the Rigi.

times happy, sometimes obscene. The women sat around the bonfires watching the mares roast in the flames. One could hear the young men's spirited horses neighing in the background. In addition, the sharp, polished spearheads shining in the moonlight cast a spell over the scene.

The fiesta lasted three days. The men ran races and played cards, jacks (*payana*), and Indian hockey (*choeca*) to pass whatever free time they had left after the quest for the Walichú and the nocturnal dancing. The young women spent their time looking happy and showing off their tiny ornamental mirrors, their glass beads, and the blue and red shawls I had given them as presents. The grey-haired warriors, on the other hand, sharing stories among themselves from past campaigns, sat apart from the women, who were deemed unworthy of listening to the tales of these feats. Meanwhile, the old women sang as they cooked. Their lyrics were filled with banter. Their saucy epigrams caused a commotion among those who heard and understood them.

At daybreak on the fourth day, the ritual murders of bulls and mares began. The strapped victims rolled about as they bellowed pitifully without arousing the slightest bit of compassion from the slaughterers, who cut their bellies open, ruthlessly pulled out their hearts, tossed their still bubbling blood towards the heavens, and implored favors from God. Drenched in blood, the almost naked slaughterers ran in front of their victims, sprinkling them with liquor or filling their mouths with tender grass of the kind the animals most favored in life. The deafening cries of spectators grew louder once the sacrificed carcasses were cast into the river. Finally, at the conclusion of the bloody ceremony, once my friends were convinced that God would grant them abundance, along with happiness in their journeys and in their Mapuche family life, we returned to the nearby camp and the orgy began.

In an attempt to temper his drunkenness with a measure of solemnity, Chacayal had changed into an outfit looted in Chile. It consisted of a red vest, a small *chiripá* (a blanket used as pants), and a woman's green robe. On his head, he wore a Chilean straw hat with a ribbon bearing an emblem and the slogan, "Long live the Argentine Confederacy, death to the savage Unitarians." Chacayal had brought this garment from the Río Colorado in his youth and had kept it as a memento of General Rosas. He assumed Rosas was my friend.

In an alcohol-induced state of agitation, the Indians once again started murmuring in a way that made me quite uneasy. I retreated to a nearby woodland. There I remained for three days in the company of my assistant and two elders whom the Indians, intoxicated as they were, had marked for death as sorcerers or "*brujos.*" Only after I learned the Indians were no longer in a condition to hurt me did I return to camp. My friend Shaihueque was sitting on the ground crying. His woman, Fia, was pouring buckets of water over his head to ward off congestion and comfort him for the loss of his last wife, Cheleukchen, a Tehuelche, who had run off after getting a harsh beating. We exchanged greetings by calling each other "Toros," (bulls, for bravery), and I laid him over my *recado* (gaucho saddle). At one point, while the totally drunken Indians were busy squabbling, I seized the opportunity to replace the *aguardiente* liquor with fresh water. To Fia's relief –she was afraid that before the drinking spree was over they'd end up burning down the camp– they continued to drink water as if it were hard liquor. The next morning the celebration was over and two days later I said good-bye to Shaihueque. I set off for the border in a hurry, thinking of the tragic events the future had in store.

Trouble was brewing and the tribespeople were jittery. No sooner had I crossed the Collón-Curá river again, than I fell into the hands of a couple of chieftains lying in wait near their camp. They were Praillan and Llofquen, whose father, chief Huiliqueupú (meaning Flintstone from the South), had gone to Buenos Aires to make a peace treaty, that is, a rationing agreement to ensure the provision of cows and mares. However, according to his sons, he had fallen victim to government witchcraft and died.

When we once again arrived at the Limay valley, we found herds of cattle that had been rustled up from *estancias* in Buenos Aires to be sold in Chile. I counted as many as one hundred and twenty rows. Indeed, the cattle rustling "business" was as ancient as it was thriving. This was also the main reason why Indian raids were so frequent. The herds were being driven by women, since the men were needed for the great invasion being planned in Salinas Grandes. I learned of this imminent danger when I stopped at Chichinal, near the area where the city of Roca is located today, as I have mentioned before. There, we ran into a group of Indians taking a break. I introduced myself as a Chilean cattle-buyer and we struck up a conversation. One of them stood out from the rest, a taciturn Indian who commanded a degree of respect from the others. We talked.

"Were a lot of Christians killed?," I asked.

"A lot, including a military commander," he said.

"Do you know his name?," I asked.

"Yes, Turao," he said.

Poor Major Jurado! We had said good-bye in Azul months before. As we parted, he had told me he feared for my life, to which I had responded: "Who knows which one of us will be killed first?"

That same Indian informed me of the death of the mail post commander from Bahía Blanca, Calderón, a kind and brave man whom I have mentioned before. I also learned about the slaughter of a beautiful young woman who had hidden under a wagon to avoid capture. I had good reason to believe these heinous acts were soon going to be repeated. It became imperative that I warn the defenseless frontier communities of the impending attack. Since I did not have enough horses to reach Patagones in time, I decided to round up the ones the Indians were using.

We saddled up our horses slowly, so as not to arouse suspicion. Meanwhile, my helper, a burly man who was the only white in our party, taking advantage of a moment's distraction on the part of the taciturn Indian, managed to hide the

Indian's saddlebag under our riding gear. Upon later examination, we discovered that the Indian was actually a "Machi" or medicine man.[7] Once on horseback, we rounded up the remaining horses and drove off with them at full speed. Almost all the Indians scrambled to their feet. Some even took off after us in hot pursuit, but the lancing of their spears ceased after I fired a few shots from my revolver in the right direction.

It was late at night when we stopped, ten leagues from Chichinal. We now had twenty-five horses in addition to our own. This made the journey to Carmen de Patagones not only possible, but also almost trouble-free. As we galloped, we could not stop thinking of the border inhabitants, who were unaware of the brutal threat that awaited them. A one-day stop to switch horses and we were back on the saddle. Two days later I arrived in Bahía Blanca and headed north again, riding day and night without taking a rest. I was lucky to have a good mount. Shaihueque had given me a hardy and handsome animal that I had reserved for the final stretch. Another horse, acquired in Patagones, was quite a good match, but had been mortally wounded in Bahía Blanca.

One afternoon I saw the exact spot where the now prosperous city of Tres Arroyos is located. In those days the only sign of life was a cabin under construction that housed the police force. At that point my horse abruptly stopped and collapsed just like the previous one. I walked up to the cabin by myself and got the necessary gear. The following day I was ready to move on. There was no time to lose, as I had to reach the telegraph post and send a message to the War Minister, alerting him of the imminent invasion.

I wondered if any of the Basques from "La Juanita," an *estancia* where I had once stopped, were still alive. Would they remember the man who had asked them for water and

---

[7] Among other objects, we found a hollow wooden tube like the ones formerly used to store stick matches. It was full of nails clipped from Indians killed in battle.

yelled out from the hitching post that terrible raids were coming their way? The De la Canal brothers often looked back on the day I warned them. I merely stopped to request a change of mount and hurriedly left. They responded by saying, "We may be able to save the family but as far as the cattle go..." They did in fact save the family, but the cattle were taken by the Indians a week later. The Basques from "La Juanita" resisted, and I think some of them lost their lives. These thoughts were on my mind as I approached the town of Tandil. It was carnival Sunday, and we still had three leagues to go, but our horses had had enough, so we were forced to stop by a water hole. It was pitch dark and we had lost our way. We made camp under a cluster of pampas grass.

As I lay down I thought of the nearby town where people were no doubt having fun, without a care in the world, their peaceful existence, at one time cut short by the Catriel uprisings, having been restored. Doctor Alsina, the War Minister, was on a mission to advance the boundary lines in anticipation of troops marching over the Río Negro. The brave General Lavalle was going to descend upon the Indians on their own frontlines. Meanwhile, a sudden Indian raid was expected in the west. However, I had evidence that it would actually take place in the south. Tandil was to become a place of mourning!

I dozed off but my imagination got carried away like a tidal wave sweeping across the events of my life. In my dreams I was a child. As I am writing this, I remember my father who in this very place, (the Moreno country manor), read us a romance about a chivalrous hero, which opens as follows:

"*On a spirited horse rides a young warrior*
Covered with hard steel and full of fervent zeal
He carries his sword under his belt; he carries a spear in its
                                                    [sheath
On his forehead there's hope and in his eyes courage..."

The morning star shone through the pampas grass, lighting up the path and the outline of the sierras. We hopped on our horses and made it to Tandil at sunrise. Anxious to deliver my message, I woke up the justice of the peace and warned him. Then I requested more horses in order to go on to Las Flores. While they were being readied I visited the loose rock. For a while I was able to breathe easily, calmly. Reluctantly, I faced reality again and got back on the saddle. I galloped day and night. Another half hour and I was in Rauch asking for more horses, without success. There were some at a nearby *estancia,* but by the time I arrived it was ten o'clock at night and everyone was asleep. My call was answered by a voice: "Take the ones in the corral." I did, but my riding skills were fairly poor and my strained legs were slow to react to a spooked horse, so I took the tenth fall of my journey. All that was left of my glasses was half a lens. Luckily, it was not a dark night. In any case, we had to reach Las Flores. Doctor Alsina was leaving Buenos Aires that night and I had to be there in time to warn him of the looming danger.

I finally made it to Las Flores in time to catch the train. I telegraphed a message to my family and boarded the train right away, no time to clean up. Stinky and raggedy as I was, my saddle weighing on me, too late to load it in the baggage compartment, I opened the door of the passenger car. Two distinguished ladies from Buenos Aires addressed me by saying, "Sir, you're in the wrong place; this is first class." I smiled at them and, swathed in my Pampa style poncho, headed for a corner hoping they would forgive the bold intruder. I perked up my ears as they talked.

"Poor Moreno, it seems the Indians have taken him captive in the Cordillera and are mistreating him. That's the word from Chile," said one.

"Forgive me, ladies, but that's not exactly the case," I interrupted. They looked at me in disbelief.

"And how do you know?"

"Because I am Moreno!" At that point we struck up a

friendly conversation, which helped pass the time. They were both friends of my sister's.

As soon as we arrived in the city I asked that the War Minister be informed immediately of the imminent Indian attack. However, I could not head off disaster. "To them, you're just a frightened little boy," one person told me that same night. Three days later the Indians raided and caused havoc. Hundreds of people died and hundreds of thousands of heads of cattle were lost. Unfortunately, I have often been disappointed, when, after a job well done, I have come back to share my findings with the pertinent authorities, as will be shown later on.

The expedition had yielded few museum pieces. Still, I was not dissapointed as the virtually untouched stretch of open country I had visited offered many an opportunity for research and an outlet for my creativity and enthusiasm.

"Dear Sirs: I would like to express my gratitude to those who have been good enough to give me this token of appreciation. As I am not used to speaking in public, I merely wish to express my acceptance of this beautiful display of friendship as an encouragement for me to persevere in my career, in hopes of being useful to my country and to the Scientific Society that has welcomed me with open arms. I hope to continue earning the appreciation of my friends, who have so clearly demonstrated that they are not indifferent to my work. A toast to the homeland, to the Argentine Scientific Society and to my friends!"[8]

---

[8] Dr. Moreno's speech at the banquet held for him upon his return from his travels.

APPENDIX

PART ONE

Letter Number 1

LETTER TO HIS FATHER
FRANCISCO FACUNDO MORENO

Azul, April 5, 1875

My Dear Old Man:

Last night when I came back from the Pinedo's estancia, where I had gone to examine the state of my skull collection before shipping it off to Buenos Aires, I received letters from all of you. I am no longer on edge now that I have news from Buenos Aires after two weeks of silence.

In my previous letter I said I was leaving for Buenos Aires on the second or third, but I could not make it because my work needed a few finishing touches. I will be headed for Tandil the day after tomorrow and plan to stay there for two days.

I don't think I will be able to assemble the total number of skulls I set out to get, but I am sure I will have 70 by tomorrow. I am sending out a case with 17 by stagecoach today, hoping you will have it picked up as soon as possible. The agent in charge of the crate has no idea what type of goods it contains.

Under other circumstances, I would have been able to satisfy my desires, but with the Indians carrying on like this, it's impossible.

I don't think it will be long, though, before I get the bones of the whole Catriel family. I already have the skull belonging to the famous Cipriano, and his wife Margarita's complete skeleton. Now it seems that Marcelino, the younger brother, doesn't have much time to live, since he is the leader of the current uprising. His beloved brother Juan José surrendered yesterday to Lavalle's Remingtons at the Nievas stream, and is expected to turn him in just as he once betrayed Cipriano. I met Juan José at a conference. He seemed to be an uncouth Indian and somewhat of a scoundrel.

With much pleasure, I read an article by Estanislao Zeballos,* and an account of Cipriano Catriel's murder. I've also talked to some people here who knew him and agree with what Estanislao has to say.

I'm holding on to the head (Catriel's). I just looked in on it and it still exudes a foul odor even though I cleaned it up a bit. I will take it with me to Tandil. I do not want to part with this gem, which is the envy of many.

In a telegram transcribed by Josué I read about old Burmeister's resignation from the Directorship of the Academy. It is surely a great loss for his students but I'm glad because now he will get some rest and prolong his life, which was being cut short each day on account of the irritations that go with his job. I've always told him he should resign.

Here in my room, I have a few small plants from Bahía Blanca and Olavarría, which I'm planning to bring to our country retreat.9

They may be of little significance, but they will always be of interest to me, because they come from the soil of the Pampas.

My best regards to all.

Affectionately,

F. P. MORENO

---

* Translator's note: Zeballos was an argentine historian.

9 The old "Quinta Moreno" (the Moreno's country manor) was located between Calle Brasil and Caseros and between Catamarca and Deán Funes. It currently houses the Bernasconi Institute. The majestic "Aguaribay" a tree planted by Moreno in front of his "mini-museum" adorns its garden.

Letter Number 2

LETTER TO HIS FATHER

———————

Bahía Blanca, October 6, 1875

My Dear Old Man:

I am writing from Bahía Blanca for the last time, taking advantage of the fact that the "Santa Rosa" steamship suffered a breakdown here. I am leaving early tomorrow morning for the Nueva Roma ruins, ten leagues west of here, where Olivieri was killed. If I find something interesting I will stay for the whole day. Otherwise I will proceed to Salinas Grandes, 8 leagues southwest of Nueva Roma, and spend the night there. This remote area has never been visited by any halfway-educated person from our country. Claráz is the only scientist who has seen it, and he tells me it is well worth visiting. From there I will set off towards the Cuyuqueo wetlands, presumably located between Salinas and the Río Colorado, and then on towards Rincón de la Espuela, where the recently subdued Indian chiefs' camps are found. My next stop after that will be Mercedes, a small fort on the Colorado. Hope to be there on the afternoon of the 12th in time to catch the Patagones-to-Bahía Blanca messenger, so I can send you my latest news. If by any chance I don't make it to that spot as planned, you'll get my letters on November 8th or 10th. I bought a pair of horses for me and my companions: two police officers and two armed Indian friends who will be helping me out on this trip. The authorities are unable to provide transportation. This trip will cost more money than I previously thought, so please send 800 pesos to Chile. I'll make a 200-peso drawing when I get to Patagones. As the steamship will be going by way of the Colonia dam, it would be good to send the clothes and the other items, as well as your letters, through the Scientific Society, but please do also send mail on the galley to Patagones.

The day before yesterday I was in Punta Alta, often mentioned by Darwin, where I picked up some artifacts that I packed off to you in two small cases and one bundle containing an armadillo shell full of specimens. Rubado will deliver them to you. Tell Zeballos I am not sending any objects to the Scientific Society. I'd have to classify them in advance for them to be of any use, which is impossible right now since I haven't got the time. Drop everything off at our place in the country, separate from my other artifacts, so they won't get mixed together.

As you can imagine, I am happy and eager to see you as soon as possible once I make the overland crossing. I will do my best to meet my objectives so I can be home at Florida 128 to celebrate my 24th birthday.

I am not writing to the others for lack of time. Tell Josué to meet with Levalle,[10] *who will tell him what this is all about. I will write to everyone from Patagones. Don't be concerned if you have no news for a while. If I find something interesting in the Pampas I might stay on for a few days...*

If possible, please send me some plants through the Scientific Society. They will enable me to earn the good will of the Justice of the Peace in Patagones.

Best regards,

FRANCISCO P. MORENO

---

[10] Marcos Levalle was well-liked by Moreno.

Letter Number 3

LETTER TO HIS FATHER

_____

Mercedes Fort, Colorado River Bank, October 13, 1875

My Dear Old Man:

As you probably read in my letter from the sixth or heard from Marcos Levalle, I left on the seventh to come here. Levalle must have told you what my escorts and I looked like when we left Bahía. One would have to leaf through Doré's illustrations of Don Quijote in order to find a more ludicrous image. To give you an idea, your Pangolín[11] wore a poncho, linen trousers, worn out boots, and had a bag hanging from his shoulder. He was riding an old bay horse for which he had paid 400 pesos. Two policemen accompanied him, who looked rather like newspaper boys (they were young), along with two wretched Indians mounted on a pair of undernourished horses with arched backs, ten times leaner than Josué's trotter. The extra horses (one per person) were even worse than the ones we were riding. I had to buy one more at a place called Nueva Roma.

On that day we rode till sunset, at which time we arrived at the above-mentioned spot, a mere ten leagues from Bahía. The going was rough and the scraggy beasts could barely gallop. At noon we broke for a lunch of "matambre" meat. The area where we ate was known as an Indian stopping place, as evidenced by the great number of horse bones scattered around in the tall grass and by the ruins from two estancias raided by my so-called "friends."

From there, the road passes through a salt marsh where only a few deer are seen from time to time. Here and there one might also see a lone mare that has strayed from the herd or maybe a traveler cast it aside. Amazingly enough, given my skill with horses, I managed to round up two of these creatures to take along with us in case we needed them for food. Between the camping spot and Nueva

---

[11] Moreno's father nicknamed him Pangolín.

Roma, the land becomes even more picturesque in spite of the salt marshes. Geologically, one can observe that the valley is lodged between two hills. It used to be an old riverbed, as wide as the Paraná, now represented by the Sauce Chico stream. The soil is extremely poor, especially in the foothills, where the tuco-tucos* have made a bad situation worse by damaging the vast dry "guadales"** stretching across several leagues of land. I climbed up a hill to look at a lion's lair, but I swear I'll never do so again unless I have good reason. The so-called Nueva Roma camp is actually the edge of a waterless streambed. Ten National Guardsmen are stationed there together with twenty Indians. They sleep out in the open with no tents or shacks to shelter them from the rain. You could say these people are doomed. In the event of an Indian raid, not a soul would survive.

Since my people and the horses were tired, I decided to stay there all day while we regained our strength somewhat. I took advantage of the occasion to study the landscape and visit the ruins adjacent to Nueva Roma, the town founded by Olivieri before his life was cut short. The ruins consist of a hillside cavern and a deep pit dug into the limestone. They end in a spacious room with a well that was used as a cell back then. This hole, according to the soldiers I met in the lowlands, holds the truth about what impelled Olivieri's people to rebel, as indeed they did on the very day two soldiers were scheduled to be shot. Olivieri, as you know, was killed in bed. The priest who was to give confession to the prisoners met the same fate.

Some soldiers say that wretched hole is haunted by a mysterious bird that was being held captive in a room and managed to escape without opening the door. Some believe it was the priest's soul, but I've seen it with my own eyes, and it is a falcon.

Early in the morning of the ninth we set off for Salinas Chicas. We took the long way, choosing a path never used by travelers before. I favored it over the trail that goes straight from Bahía to the Colorado, since I needed to get accustomed to danger. Neither path

---

*   Translator's note: Argentine rodent.
** Translator's note: Sandy bogs.

is completely safe, though. We heard in Bahía Blanca that there was more to fear along this unknown track to Patagones than along the road from there to Chile. I was allured nonetheless, since I was about to satisfy my curiosity.

The path to Salinas is atrocious but nonetheless intriguing. At the far end of a saltpan I saw a grove of carob trees, sombra de toro trees (Jodina Rhombifolia) chañar trees (Geoffroea Decorticans) and other trees as well, which made it well worth the trouble to get there. Past this woodland there is a three-league stretch of very high dunes that one must cross before getting to Salinas. We barely made it there by 1 p.m., even though it's only six leagues away from Roma. At every turn, I thought about the odds of being attacked by Indians, who were most surely there. Luckily, we merely ran into their tracks. Salinas Chicas is a pretty sight. There is good, grassy ground cover, and there are sources of fresh spring water on its outskirts. What makes the landscape dazzle, though, are the alfalfa fields, so high and so green, one would think they were purposely cultivated. These plants, the work of nature alone, are more beautiful than any alfalfa field in Buenos Aires.

By now the horses were pretty traveled out, so I let them eat while I collected soil and salt samples. That night we woke up in a panic after we heard a noise. It must have been the Indians passing through near the sand dunes. They probably didn't see us in the tall grass where we slept. At 6 a.m. on the 10th we were once again on horseback headed towards Las Escobas. We arrived at 10 a.m. and stayed until 1 p.m. for the sake of the bedraggled horses. We had to kill a mare to eat, since the two Indians, taking advantage of an inattentive moment on my part, devoured the last of our provisions, consisting of my "matambre" meat and bread. After these two ingrates gobbled up everything and finished off the sugar, they refused to continue accompanying me. Their excuse was that the horses were so thin, they'd never make it to the Colorado. Since I wanted to get rid of them without having the commanding officer of Bahía Blanca conclude that I wasn't appreciative of the escort, I immediately sent them on their way. Now I am writing to him so he'll throw them in jail for 15 days.

After eating barbecued mare (I can't understand why people find it disgusting, since it's so delicious) and an armadillo, the two police officers and I struck out towards Las Calaveras, 12 leagues from Las Escobas. There we found water for the horses and firewood to last us through the night. At about 6 p.m. that day we were scared out of our wits once more at the sight of people in the distance. With our horses too worn out to run and the sorry state of my men's weaponry –consisting of two carbines in worse shape than the ones Schindler sent to our place in the country– we knew we were in trouble. I, personally, was well armed, but I would not have been up to the challenge of defending myself against 15 or 20 men. The only ones who tread these parts are Indians under Picún's command, and he spares no one. However, night soon fell so they didn't see us. We calmly proceeded along our way until we reached Las Calaveras at 10 p.m. With nothing to eat –the slaughtered mare had decomposed in the heat– we were forced to an early start on the 11th in hopes of reaching the Colorado that same day. We arrived at 5p.m. I passed through a small fort along the way, Fort Romero Grande, an extraordinarily dangerous place on account of the Indians. Their spear marks are sliced into the walls. The roof of the kitchen, once made out of hay, is burnt, and holes perforate the room that served as a fort.

The Indians have wreaked this havoc in hopes that the Christians will not be able to defend themselves or take shelter in that place. When I arrived, it was evident from the spear marks that eight Indians had been there some time before. It is here in Romero Grande and in Monte Callao that Indians attack travelers. One can see clothes and an occasional cross marking the burial site of a hapless victim.

The Mercedes fort, on the Colorado, from where I am now writing you, is commanded by a dark-skinned captain named Alvarado. He fed me and served me a cup of tea with milk as soon as I arrived. It felt good, after going 30 hours on an empty stomach. Captain Alvarado said that Commander Bernal[12] was due any moment en

---

[12] Bernal: General Liborio Bernal, well-liked and admired by Moreno, was his good friend and a great patriot who went out of his way to help Moreno get to Nahuel Huapi.

*route to a conference at Cacique Queupumil's, three leagues away.
I decided to wait for him so I could participate in this event, which
would follow the chief's wedding celebration. Then I could proceed
with Bernal on the trip to Patagones.*

*Bernal arrived yesterday afternoon and is taking a nap here in
the bedroom. He says everything will work out fine. If the Indians
(from the tribes friendly with Linares) refuse to go home, he says
that under the pretext of a government commission, he will send
them with me to Las Manzanas, where I won't run the risk of losing my life or of being taken captive. In that way, I might be able to
send a telegram from Chile soon, perhaps in late February or early
March. Bernal is taking a great interest in my work, and I am certain he will do everything possible to ensure its success.*

*I am enclosing a rough sketch of the trip we made. It's the best I
could do given the lack of good pens, or even a ruler or compass.
Besides there's so much sand I can't keep anything clean. Save it
because when I get back I may need it if I lose my papers.*

*I was able to collect a few items on this trip, including land
snails, sand samples, and stones from the hills. By the way, the day
before yesterday when I arrived, I was standing at the door of the
fort looking at the pit and saw what appeared to be human bones.
When I pulled them up, they turned out to be an Indian skeleton,
though incomplete and badly broken. I forwarded it with my luggage in a wagon bound for Patagones that Bernal has filled with
gifts for the Indians. I will stay with him until the 19th so I can see
some of the area and wait for letters from you in response to the one
I sent by stagecoach.*

*We are well taken care of at this fort. Milk comes straight from
the cow. We have tea with milk and good mare-meat cutlets, even
though they are served without potatoes. I haven't had a potato
since I left Las Flores. I also have a good bed, but I'm anxious to get
to Chile soon.*

*Bernal has asked me for some plants to fix up a small farm he
bought in Patagones, where he is getting married on the 23rd of this
month to one of Benito Crespo's granddaughters. Send me some
through the "Society," especially casuarinas (Australian pine), and
some nice flowering plants. I don't think the "Santa Rosa" will be*

coming to Patagones any time soon, after running aground and wrecking in Bahía Blanca. I don't even know if it has departed from there yet.

Tell Josué that rather than sending me 5 pounds of coffee beans he should send twelve and a half pounds ground. Good coffee won't taste bad even if I run out of sugar. As for tea, 5 pounds is enough. Also send some eucalyptus seeds so I can plant them in Nahuel Huapi to mark a trail.

I couldn't be in better health. I just had a minor headache on the day I arrived, but finding the Indian bones cured it completely. My body is in excellent shape even after galloping 40 leagues. I am stronger than I thought.

My next letter posted from Patagones will bring news of the event scheduled for the day after tomorrow, which promises to be grand. We've already had six Indian delegations come, announcing that they are our "good friends," they are "good-hearted," and that "so and so is happy," etc. It is quite annoying to me, particularly because they won't let me measure their heads.

Let me know how my museum is doing and if you have picked up the condor bones and the lion from the embalmer. Tell Juanita and Maruja[13] not to worry. Though I'm darker than Cruz and reek of colt oil, I'm in better health than in Buenos Aires, and I'm certain I will soon see them again. Also tell Josué and Eduardo,[14] Reid and Zeballos[15] that I will write from Patagones. However, advise Zeballos not to publish anything about the trip.

I hope all is well with you. Affectionately, your son,

FRANCISCO P. MORENO

---

[13] Juanita and Maruja are his sisters.
[14] Eduardo is his brother.
[15] Zeballos: Doctor Estanislao Zeballos.

Letter Number 4

LETTER TO HIS FATHER

———————————

Patagones Fort, October 23, 1875

My Dear Old Man:

A moment ago I received your nice letter from the 10th. It was a relief to hear from you after such a long time. The post is so unreliable here, one never knows. If you get this letter soon, don't forget that the galley to Bahía Blanca sails on the 10th or 11th. If you send things to Carinti, as you have in the past, I won't have any problems getting them by messenger. I am keen to hear from you as soon as possible before I start out on the big exploration.

I am assuming you received my letter from the Río Colorado dated the 13th of this month and that you were impressed by my visit to Salinas Chicas, etc. I wrote that I was about to take part in an Indian "parliament" or get together. In fact, it was held on the 15th and 16th. Groups of Indian delegates made up of the children and close relatives of the caciques started arriving the day before. When you look at the contrast between the shabby clothes these tribesmen wear and the way they flaunt their magnificent silver daggers, stirrups, and spurs, it makes you wonder. The first thing they did upon entering the room where we waited was shake hands, the right hand, on behalf of their parents. They recited a long speech in Araucanian about how joyful their chiefs were, to the point of having been up all night from the excitement of the upcoming assembly and salutation.

On the 15th we had an early lunch. At 10 a delegation arrived, waving a white flag and announcing that the "Cacique General" was on his way to the site of the ceremony. Bernal sent us there on horseback and gave us each a firecracker to explode in front of our audience as we passed in front of it. I was riding the famous "Bahía Blanca Harp," and hoped it wouldn't dare become defiant during this important engagement.

We set off at 12; there were 57 of us including officers, soldiers, friendly Indians and myself. The designated site was a large turn-around, free from quicksand and dominated by a red willow. For this reason I aptly named it "The Lone Willow Parliament." It was roughly twenty cuadras *from the starting point. The caciques weren't there yet when we arrived. Bernal and I took our place in front, together with the officers and 10 soldiers. Behind us stood 40 young men from a tribe that was friendly with Linares.*

Fifteen minutes later the Indian contingent approached us and raced around the area three times to the tune of infernal shouting. Leading the party was Cacique General Queupumil, somewhat tipsy and dressed in a red jacket with gilded ornamental fasteners gifted to him by Bernal. His chieftains and able-bodied men followed behind. They were riding magnificent horses that were cleaner than their owners. The "troops" were armed with lances and divided into units, each commandeered by chieftains, just like we were. This battalion, regiment or squadron was composed of 130 Indians who were true devils. Güenupil followed closely behind. He was a very good cacique *who had brought 89 Indians. Then came Yancamil, another* cacique, *with 74. All in all there were 293. While they were circling around, we stepped back from the scene, which, in its splendor, evoked memories of "The Lunar Dwellers," except that these masks were a hundred times better and truly natural. One of the chieftains, who later told me he was a "speaker," carried a* quillango *fur tied around his neck and wore a clownish headdress. He was armed with a saber, longer than the one Fierabrás thrust at him as they both engaged in swordplay. They made stabbing motions with their weapons every which way. Another man, who was without a saber, had a broken* facón *(large knife) instead. It was tied to a willow branch with which he brandished the most bizarre figures. The rest of the Indians copied them as they played with their long spears, turning their horses to the right and to the left amid shrieks that spooked our horses.*

The music was sublime. There was a dented trumpet, a large cane wrapped in leather with holes drilled into it and a bull's horn on top. It was probably used for bugle calls but resounded like the endless brays of a donkey. I couldn't begin to tell you about everything that happened that day because it would be a very long story and I wouldn't be able to relate even a tenth of it in the forty-five minutes I have left to finish this letter. When they concluded their rounds, it was time for us to do likewise. Unfortunately, one of the soldiers started detonating firecrackers beside me, frightening my horse. If I had not quickly broken ranks, my horse would surely have pitched and I would have taken a bad fall. Since I wanted to conduct my expedition, rather than get hurt and stay in Colorado for good, I waited until the others had rounded the third lap before I joined them again.

That done, the formal salutation began. The Cacique General's *party went first. The greeting consists primarily in using one's right hand to shake everyone else's right hand. The salute starts at the left and then goes back around in similar manner for a good-bye handclasp. The words "mari-mari Peñi Huinca" (How are you Christian brother?), etc., etc. were repeated incessantly. It's quite fastidious, because you have to give more than three hundred hand-shakes while on horseback. Sometimes it can turn downright dangerous when the Indian being greeted is drunk and prone to remain locked in an embrace, causing an unskilled rider like myself to lose his balance. It didn't help that I was wearing glasses either, which made me stand out among the others.*

After greeting the three caciques from the three parties and their respective chieftains in this manner, we said our good-byes and headed for the fort to wait until the next day's parliament. The fur-clad speaker, Santerre, (he was the spitting image of the famous lover of Marie Antoinette), Yancamil and the numerous other chieftains, all of whom looked more like toads than humans, presented the agenda. But I don't have time to go into details right now. I will tell you about it and about the journey from the Río Colorado in my next letter. I'll also write about the expedition to Punta Rasa and Bahía San Blas, scheduled to begin Monday. Suffice it to say that I've galloped 13 hours straight, covering 31 leagues. Oddly enough, my body doesn't feel a thing, although I slept in my saddle on a plank all night. I must be very strong! People around me are indeed stunned, as they never expected I would turn out to be so resilient. Today I had no time to eat, so busy was I writing to you all. I started at two and it's already 7:25. My fingers are stiff.

I am expecting certain items that you should be sending through the Society to Patagones. (If you do, make sure Patagones is in fact the first stop, because if it is Chubut I may be stuck here waiting for a month.) As soon as I get them I'll be on my way to Chile. I'd like to be at Choele-Choel Island on your birthday. I am planning to leave on the 15th, if possible, but when you write back please send your letters via the galley that leaves there on the 10th or 11th of November. Bernal's messenger will deliver them to me. I'll write to you before I take off. Allow me to instruct Josué as to how the funds should be allocated: Please wire 250 pesos or so, because I need to bring along food supplies for me and the rest of the people. Manuel Linares has finally decided he's coming along, although somewhat unwillingly according to Cruzado, since the 10,000 pesos fall short of his expectations. Bernal has come through for me like the good friend that he is, arranging everything in accordance with the written instructions from Alsina that Solé provided.[16] This has helped us get government funding for the trip.

In light of the circumstances, Pops, there's no need to worry. Your son will be back at Saint Christopher's Eden[17] for the holy day of Saint Pascasio, full of pride and glory, because his father has taught him so well how to steer his natural talents in the right direction. With Linares at my side, there's nothing to be afraid of. The Indians won't dare cause trouble, as Linares is their friend and is related to the major caciques. Besides, I am bringing some mares as gifts for the Indians (Now I've become a herdsman.) Bernal is sending them to Shaihueque.

I'm running out of time. Hope to hear from you soon. Hugs and kisses to Pilotín,[18] and hug Fanny[19] for me.

Don't worry about me and take care of yourself until my return.

FRANCISCO P. MORENO

As soon as I post this one I'll go back to Bernal's wedding. Please keep a tight lid on the Linares matter.

---

[16] Solé: Married to his sister Juana.
[17] The Moreno country manor.
[18] His brother Daniel's nickname.
[19] Fanny Gowland, his father's second wife.

Letter Number 5

LETTER TO HIS FATHER

_____

Patagones Fort, November 11, 1875

My Dear Old Man:

I received all of your letters and the materials I requested. They came on the "Santa Rosa" on the eighth and last night through the "Society." Now, as soon as our horses eat the tender grass that has sprung up after the rains and get their strength back, we'll head towards Choele-Choel and the Indian camps of Rauqueucurá, Shaihueque, Inacayal, Nahuel Huapi Lake and Chile. I may be able to send you a letter with the date of my departure when the steamship sails on the 15th or 16th.

I haven't done much since I wrote to you on the 25th. I've been held back by foul weather and the need to make travel arrangements. I've only made one trip to Bahía San Blas, where I spent 6 days working quite productively for the Scientific Society, our Moreno "Eden," and my own museum. I'm shipping you a case of onion plants on the steamship. Some of these plants were growing over an Indian cemetery in Bahía San Blas; the rest are from Punta Rasa.

The plants you sent arrived in perfect condition. They now adorn Bernal's property. He asked me to thank you profusely. Presently, we're getting ready to sow some of the seeds you sent so that Patagones will bear a resemblance to the Botanical Garden of Caseros St.[20] Bernal will make the delivery arrangements for an Araucaria from the farm belonging to his wife's grandfather. I'll pick up some seeds from the pine-covered foothills and send them to you. I'm writing long letters to everyone from the steamship, especially you, following up on my letter from the 25th. I'll do the same via the "Society."

_____

[20] The Moreno country manor (Quinta Moreno).

Don't forget to write to Valdivia. I want to have a ton of letters when I get there. Since I may not be looking exactly like a "dandy" when I arrive in town, there's a chance I could be taken for a freak going by the name of "Dr. Pangolín," so it wouldn't be a bad idea for you to send a photograph of me to the Argentine Consul in the region. The plates are at Loudet's and were taken in late July or early August 1874, before the journey to Santa Cruz.

Regards to all my family and friends. Tell everyone to rest assured and not to worry. Maybe you'll hear from me when I get to Valdivia, less than four months from now.

I know I don't need to explain myself to you. You know me and understand that I won't subject myself to anything more than what's necessary to ensure the success of this expedition, which will make me famous among my compatriots and provide a wealth of knowledge. That is all I ask for.

Your son,

FRANCISCO P. MORENO

Letter Number 6

LETTER TO HIS FATHER

_____

Patagones Fort, November 16, 1875

My Dear Old Man:

Our letters must have crossed in the mail. I received the three you sent via the steamship and the "Society," which were posted on the same date as the ones I mailed you. On the 11ᵗʰ I wrote to tell you I'd send you a long letter via the "Santa Rosa" with news of my travel plans.

My letter dated October 23 ended off on the Saturday of the preliminary assembly called into session by the Colorado chiefs.

On Saturday the 16ᵗʰ we had an early meal, as we suspected our honorable guests would want to honor us by having us partake in their fast. Around 9:30 we sighted the big chief's entourage south of the river. He had sent a delegation to ascertain whether we were ready. A makeshift white flag was raised in the form of a thoroughly worn-out shirt. In reply, the fort hoisted a towel on the end of a spear. This signaled that people were friendly, inviting the delegates to approach, which they did. The delegates looked like extraterrestrials in carnival attire. The band of musicians also sounded like something from outer space. Each Indian held a shiny spear. When they were about one hundred and thirty feet from the fort they stopped. A speaker stepped forward accompanied by two Indians and shouted at the top of his lungs that the Great Chief Queupumil, General of the Colorado Territory, would soon pay a visit to commanding officer Bernal.

The reply from the fort was favorable; the chief was more than welcome. The Indians rushed back to announce the good news. At 10:15 the whole contingent started crossing the river in a display of pomp and circumstance. Heading the party were the three chiefs and a Chilean, Elías Bernal, who looked as slick as a whistle. About 60 chieftains accompanied by their strongest and bravest young men followed behind, armed with spears, sabers, and large knives. Clad in their most lavish garments, they looked more ridiculous than ever. The "Music Band," consisting of several copper and animal horns, rendered an Indian medley far richer but no less incomprehensible than Dr. Uriarte's band.

As the Indians rode into the fort courtyard, countless firecrackers, whizzers, and toe-chasers stored behind the gates went off. I've never laughed so hard. Stunned by the magnificent welcome, the Indians couldn't stop saying "nice," "nice." They ducked every time one whizzed by, thinking something was flying overhead. As ludicrous as this was, one could see they were master horsemen. In an enclosed space of roughly 90 by 30 feet there were thirty or forty of them on spirited horses, with firecrackers exploding everywhere, yet no one fell off. The meeting started at 11 in the main room of the fort, which had been fixed up with makeshift benches made of boxes and old doors. Even though the attendees were well dressed, it wasn't appropriate to give them chairs. The three chiefs, their speakers, chieftains, and the sons and uncles of these important individuals were seated on one side. Some bottles of liquor were set on a table separating us from them. We looked so serious we could have been going to a funeral.

Chief Queupumil opened the proceedings by telling Bernal, through a speaker, that he had been up all night from the excitement, that he had great happiness in his heart, and that he wanted to be his friend. Bernal kept repeating "that's good, tell him I'm his friend too." The exchange of platitudes went well, but when the requests started, the situation turned infernal. The three speakers and the famous orator Yancamil (or I should say Santerre, since both are so remarkably alike) made more of a din than a street rally. Every phrase they uttered ended in a loud sustained shout of "eceuu," followed by "pipili," to which the most important chief would reply "pipi" as a sign of concurrence. They asked for five hundred cows for each of the three chiefs, unquestionably on the advice of the Chileans, who wanted cattle to take to Chile. Queupumil and Yancamil out shouted everyone, but it was the speaker in the quillango fur that attracted attention. I've mentioned him before. Judging from the enthusiastic outburst that followed each of

his long speeches, I believe this individual's compatriots would refer to him in the same terms as Lamartine's applied to Cicero: "Cicero is not just the name of an orator, it is the name of elocution itself."
I, on the other hand, thought he was nothing more than a first-class screamer with an attitude befitting Salvoni.
After three or four hours of arguing back and forth it was decided that the chiefs would send a delegation to meet with the government in Buenos Aires. This done, the caciques said their good-byes, their arms full of gifts of firecrackers and liquor. They announced that their hearts rejoiced, but ours were beating fast, since we hadn't kept our promise to them. The obese Yancamil and I argued about the location of the circulatory system's central organ. He refused to believe it is located on the left. Stroking his belly (which is bigger than Acebal's, even though Yancamil is shorter), he indicated that the heart was located there, somewhere near the liver.
The wedding was called off because Queupumil said he was poor and couldn't afford to pay his future in-laws. What's more, Bernal did not want to be blamed if the bride committed suicide, so he played dumb. The sixteen-year-old bride-to-be, the daughter of one of Queupumil's chieftains, had threatened to hang herself if her family forced her to marry against her will. There was a precedent for this type of behavior. A poor girl had once killed herself when forced to wed Queupumil, who is 60 years old and uglier than Dr. You-Know-Who. Bernal did not try to solve Queupumil's dilemma. Suicides like these are quite frequent. It goes to show that these Indian women are not without feelings, which places them a cut above their Tehuelche counterparts to the South.
In the enclosed envelope you will find a brooch that belongs to a local sissy. This individual dresses like a man but doesn't sling bolas or do any of the manly tasks here. He just takes care of the "chinas".* Give this jewel to Maruja[21] to keep for me until I return. I

---

* Translator's note: young Indian women.
[21] Maruja, his beloved sister, often looked in on his "mini-museum." At Moreno's request, she would keep an eye on the astute Burmeister when he visited the collection, as Burmeister could barely resist the temptation of whisking away some of its paleontology specimens.

doubt there is another one like it. Its design reminds me of the jewels recently found among the ruins of Troy or of Peruvian idols
shaped like owl-faced figurines.

Bernal was in a hurry to see his bride-to-be, so on Sunday the
17th at 6 a.m. sharp, we set off from the Río Colorado heading that
way. The soil on both sides of the river all the way to Fort Viejo,
where we turned to go south, is of good quality but was under
severe strain due to the lack of rainfall. I don't think this land is as
outstanding as people say. The province of Buenos Aires has land
that's as good or even better. I wouldn't advise anyone to settle here.
It would be a risky financial endeavor, given that the Indians aren't
completely trustworthy yet. The stretch of good land is not very
wide. I don't even think it covers two leagues.

South of Fort Viejo, located five leagues from Mercedes, the land
is of very poor quality. There are sand dunes, salt marshes, and
woodland in abundance, which would at times interfere with cattle
raising. The worst drawback, however, is the long dry stretch. From
here to the next waterholes there is a distance of twelve leagues. We
arrived at one o'clock and left at two, after eating some cold barbecued mare and a hot guanaco dish. The conditions at this fort are
awful. There is no garbage pit, for one. However, in comparison
with the first waterholes, where the water makes you sick, it's a
palace. Fifteen leagues separate the two forts, each composed of a
small garrison manned by four soldiers. We got there at 8 p.m. I felt
sorry for the poor black soldier who drove the herd, working hard to
keep the horses from running away. Since I wanted to give him a
break, I was unable to make it to El Carmen that day. In addition,
my horse needed to rest. He had stumbled on a tree trunk and
almost ejected me. Luckily, I didn't break any ribs but I found
myself straddling on his neck. This is not good terrain for riding at
night, especially if the rider is half-blind. The trees are so slender
and their foliage so dense, you end up thinking the trees are Indians. It's quite daunting, but if you let them frighten you, you'll
have a very bad time. To make matters worse, crosses dot the
scenery along the way, marking the sites of the poor souls fallen victim to the Indians. This is no place for the fainthearted.

I slept comfortably over some planks inside the fort, after filling

up on mate *tea made with saltwater. I woke up at the crack of dawn
to get my horse, but found that the herd had run off driven by thirst
in search of water. There were only five horses left, mine included. I
lent one out so a rider could go look for the rest of the herd, and
headed for this town riding the worn-out nag on which I had galloped more than 25 leagues the day before. I switched horses along
the way, but the other horse gave up on me after a six-league stretch
at the site of the Walicho, a sacred Indian tree under which Darwin
found shelter in 1832. It was a march of seven leagues. Step by step,
tugging at my horse's rein for more than half the time, I arrived at
11 a.m. having endured the galloping unscathed. I must be stronger
than I thought.*

*I hung around for a few days, worked on my journals, and tried
to expedite the trip to Chile. On the 25th I set off for Bahía de San
Blas, after attending Bernal's wedding. That same night I rode into
an estancia in Punta Rasa. I stopped there for two days to gather
sand samples and a few shells; but the beach there contained scant
material for my collection.*

*From my observations so far I can surmise that most sources of
fresh water are located to the side or in between sand dunes, which
does away with the notion that all dunes are harmful. I don't think
anyone before me has noticed this. The compact soil from here to
Bahía Blanca keeps the water from stagnating. Pools form but dust
and sand storms quickly cover them. In the dunes, however, rainwa-
ter seeps through the sand all the way down to the solid layer, where
it remains impervious to the sun, whose heat cannot evaporate it. The
water is preserved in perfect condition and forms exquisite springs of
very fresh water. In areas where there are cracks, these springs are
surrounded by abundant vegetation, which also protects them from
the sun. Dig a few feet near a sand dune and you'll find an excellent
source of water. I've found water by sticking my knife one foot into
the ground. The space quickly filled up with drinking water.*

*Bahía San Blas is very picturesque but good pastureland is
scarce. Grass grows in abundance only in the space between the
sand dunes. There I picked up shells and discovered an Indian cemetery dating back to the days when sea lions were a staple of the
natives' diets. I found eight skulls, some arrows and sea lion bones,*

which I'm packing off to you in a big crate. I am sending a package with a few small onions I collected and Federico's white poncho. Rubado will deliver it to you.

Bahía San Blas is located 18 or 20 leagues from here. On the 31st at 5 a.m. I left the Punta Rasa estancia, so I could meet Bernal for lunch on the day of San Nemesio. I managed to get here at 9 a.m. after galloping for 12 leagues. I haven't left town much since my arrival. I did pay one visit to Linares at Potrero Cerrado, nine leagues from here, to make arrangements for the trip. That's mainly what I've been doing.

My travel plans have been beset by problems. If it weren't for Bernal, the trip to Chile would cost a lot of money. To begin with, Guerrico didn't handle himself very well with the Linares. Then there's a rumor, spread by mean-spirited people. They say the government has given me huge sums of money, 50,000 pesos firm. This has led Linares to reject my offer. When Bernal offered another four hundred pesos firm on behalf of the national government, Linares changed his mind. The departure was set for the 20th, but three days ago Manuel Linares sent word to Bernal that he was sick and that it wasn't worthwhile for him to risk his life for such little money.

The trip was on the verge of getting derailed, so Bernal summoned Linares's other brothers. He told one of them, Mariano, to take me because the government so ordered. Mariano, who is a very good man, finally agreed on condition that I procure the horses, saying that he didn't have any. The rascal wants to make a net profit of 20,000 pesos.

Bernal couldn't fund any more expenses. He had already informed the authorities that he had given Mariano Linares 1,000 pesos to cover the trip and the horses. Therefore, I'm going to have to pay for them. For that reason, the drawing I told you I was going to make on you from here will be 500 pesos on behalf of the "Society," rather than the 250 or 300 I mentioned to you before. I need 10 or 15 docile horses to ride. Departure is set for the 27th. I chose that day because it's your birthday. That will bring me good luck. I'll draw the money at-sight plus five days. You can send the rest to me in Valdivia for my trip back to Buenos Aires.

My next letter, whether sent through the "Society" or by post on the 24*th*, will be my last one from here. I'll include information on how to contact me. One letter with which Mr. Clark has been good enough to provide me is for a mission near Osorno, run by a missionary friend of his whose name I can't remember at the moment, but I'll tell you later. Right now I'm on a steamship that will depart in two hours. If you write to the Argentine Consul in Valdivia asking him to forward your letter (one will be enough, as there is a chance I might not make it to the mission) for that priest, I'll be able to get it when I land in Chile.

I must say that with each passing day, my confidence in the outcome of this trip grows. Bernal is doing his best to ensure that all goes well. To help achieve my goal, I've arranged for the New Year's rations to be delivered now to Chief Ñancucheo's Indians, so they won't have to wait for them and can come with me on my journey. I'll be sure to make it known to them that they have me to thank for this, so they take better care of me.

Bernal sends lots of gifts for them on behalf of the Argentine government. I'm bringing liquor, 10 fine ponchos, 10 chiripá blankets, 10 hats, 10 shirts, 10 pairs of boots, and a beautiful pair of silver stirrups for Shaihueque, etc. In addition to all this I have personal gifts for them, so there'll be a big celebration upon my arrival at the Indian camps. Bernal has also donated a magnificent sergeant major's tent, where I'll be as comfortable as if I were home at Florida 128. If the Indians want it, I won't hesitate to give it away. It will make a gift (forced though it may be) fit for a king.

Bernal is enjoying his plants and has asked me to send you a case of chacolí* wine from the winery of Dr. Benito Crespo, who is the grandfather of Bernal's wife. Bernal promises to send more and better quality wine after the first harvest. As you can see, he is not all bad, despite the fact that he's very lazy. Have a couple of glasses on the day of San Facundo. I'll drink a toast from the same batch when I set up camp that day. However, keep one bottle so we can drink it together when I arrive. If the wine is delivered now I'll send it by steamship; otherwise it'll have to wait for the "Society."

---

* Translator's note: light wine.

I'm glad you're talking to General Mitre about my work. He was instrumental to the realization of this trip. Don't think I underestimate the words he spoke at my museum, which you mention in your letter. I've been thinking about them and also reading a biography of Audubon, the North American naturalist, which Mitre was kind enough to lend me. That has been a big help to me in my expedition. If Audubon spent eleven years bird watching in the forests of North America, why can't I live among the Indians for a few months? When you see General Mitre please give him my best regards, and extend a greeting to Juan María Gutierrez, who has always encouraged me to go forward with my plans.

Please show Zeballos and Reid this letter. Tell Zeballos not to publish anything I'm telling you, especially what I say about Bernal. The government may not like what I have to say about him, and I wouldn't want to cause any harm to my good friend. When I send word from Chile, Zeballos can write something up and even go to press with it, revealing all that's being done here for me. You won't have to wait too long.

If I run into Indians that've come for their rations, I might be able to write to you along the way. Rest assured, I'll take advantage of every opportunity to send word. I'm well, so don't fret if by chance you don't hear from me until March or April.

As I told you in the letter I mailed the other day, it would be a good idea if you could send a photo of me to the Argentine Consul. I hope it comes with lots of letters. You can be sure that if I find something around here for our country estate I'll gladly send it along as my contribution to our "garden of Eden."

Goodbye for now, dear father. My best wishes to all those who remember me. You can take comfort in knowing that I will come back as soon as possible.

F. P. MORENO

If I get the case of wine, Rubado will deliver it. I'm sending you my eyeglasses. They are notable pieces of Patagonian art –the civilized kind!

Letter Number 7

LETTER TO HIS FATHER

On the road to Chile. Primera Angostura del Río Negro
December 5, 1875

My Dear Old Man:

My last letter was very short. I was in agony on account of a bad tooth. Immediately after I sealed the letters I went to see Mr. Humble, an English missionary, for help. However, after three good tugs at my tooth, he shattered it and couldn't extract it. He warned me not to touch it until I got to Chile. Now that the cavity is quite large I can use my own mixture of strong medicines to ease the pain. My toothaches never last too long or hurt too much.

My previous letter didn't mention a word about my travels. The steamship set out on the 16th. On the 18th I was on my way to Aguada de Los Loros en el Océano, 25 leagues from this small town. The first day, we stopped in San Javier to take care of a few arrangements for the trip with the Indians. One can never be too sure with these people. They always object to something or other. We spent the night there. It rained hard all night and, in the morning, the guide, other travel companions and I continued on our way to La Aguada. Unfortunately, after a six-league march we found ourselves in the middle of a rainstorm. It went on for two hours, with hailstones falling everywhere. When it stopped the waterlogged ground became a trap for our horses. Every time we tried to ride it they would sink into the quicksand up to their bellies. We kept going like this for about two leagues, tugging them by the reins, the water reaching over our knees. Every so often we'd fall into one of the millions of holes that dot this landscape. They were made by tuco-tuco rodents.

Our guide lost his way because the path was not marked. I had to walk in the rain all day on an empty stomach until 8:00 that night. We finally stopped in the dunes near the ocean. It was hard to sleep because rain kept falling on our heads. Early on the 20th we climbed a dune in order to assess our location. According to our guide we still had 10 leagues to go before reaching La Aguada. Our horses were so tired they could neither trot nor gallop. After walking for some time with no set course, I realized that our guide knew about as much as I did and that we were lost.

Luckily, I was able to enlist the aid of a compass I always carry in my pocket. Since I knew which way to go to get to the Río Negro, we gradually headed in that direction. That day (which happened to be Juanita's birthday), I had nothing to eat. I had not eaten the day before either. The water I drank was squeezed out of my poncho, which was drenched through and through because it was raining non-stop. After a fourteen-hour trek we came upon the Lagunas de Gutierrez, a series of light brown lagoons where we set up camp for the night. We drank mate *tea, but couldn't sleep because it was still raining.*

The next morning at nine we sighted the Río Negro Valley. First we switched horses and ate some barbecued lean mare that was worse than rotten meat. Then I picked up some arrows off the ground. We made it to Carmen that night. Still, I am not complaining about the discomforts we endured. I've come to realize that getting wet doesn't make me sick, and no matter how much it pours, I know nothing will happen to me. Besides, I found an oyster fossil deposit in the hills; I also picked up a live snail and a few arrows.

Between the 22nd and the 27th I organized the freighters for the final departure. Early on the 27th I saw my horses, all 12 of them very good ones. After sending some over to Linares to lighten up my load I had lunch with Bernal, who served me a fine champagne in honor of your birthday and the trip.

At 2 p.m. I mounted and so did my assistant, Guerra, whom I will drop off in Valdivia. He was armed with a seven-round carbine given to me by Bernal. We rode along a riverbank, admiring the landscape. On one side was a great mass of rock with barely enough space in some areas for a forward-facing horse. On the other was a lovely view of islands filled with quince trees, walnuts, vineyards, and huge willows. It was enough to make the region the envy of the

*Tigre Islands or the Paraná River. Bernal rode with me for two
leagues, but had to go back because his wife was sick.*

   *In a little while I'll be going down to Guardia General Mitre to
see Bernal off. I spent the night at Mr. Vicente Herrero's, who is
Claudio Gonzalez's first cousin. He not only remembered me from
the first trip, but also gave me a nice welcome knowing of our relationship to the Gándaras. The following day I crossed four horses
south of the river and sent word to Mariano Linares that I would
be expecting him there at six in the morning. Afterwards I
resumed my travel, passing through the most picturesque area I've
ever seen in my life. Imagine a park as green as Palermo but with
bigger willows covering 20 leagues. At four in the afternoon I
arrived at La China Muerta, owned by a young Swiss, Dr. Eduardo Zeller. He is a learned man who looked after me very well. I
never expected this kind of welcome around here. It's hard to
believe that there could be people from good families in these
remote areas, many of whom have been utterly ruined by bad
crops. The Flajers, for instance, the younger sons of an English
lord and duke, have spent 20,000 pounds sterling and recovered
nothing. That's exactly what's going to happen to a certain Mr.
Enrique Grandville, who comes from a good family in England.
They are very decent people who are used to a certain standard of
living. No matter how good their crops are, they cannot meet all
their expenses.*

   *In order for you to appreciate the quality of people we're talking
about, let me tell you that with few exceptions, each of these English or Swiss farmers possesses between 400 and 500 selected liter-
ary works in their own homes. Since I had letters of introduction
from Dr. Tomás Kincaid, the owner of the house, I was immediately welcome. His brother is the engineer in charge of building the
Argentine battleship; he's the one whose arm was cut off in a hors-
ing accident. About fifteen cuadras from here live the Bucklands.
They are nephews of a famous English naturalist by the same name
who has studied prehistoric cultures in England. I always have a
good time when I go there. If not for the huge servings of plum pud-
ding, cake, and beefsteak pie I am expected to eat, I wouldn't miss
Buenos Aires one bit.*

They've shown me two Indian cemeteries, a sketch of which I am forwarding to you for safekeeping. There, I have found roughly 100 arrows and 2 skulls. In my opinion these artificial mounds are arranged in very similar manner to the ones built by prehistoric Indians. They look a lot like the ancient tombs found in Georgia, Louisiana, and New York in the United States.

I have had the opportunity of sighting three different ethnic tribes that inhabit this region: the Tehuelches, the Manzaneros, (Apple-tree people), who speak Araucanian, and the famous Pampas, whose very existence was widely doubted by all, I included. Now I know that the Querandíes were not Araucanian. There are few remnants of this population, who call themselves "Gennaken," and whose grandparents, according to an old tradition, hailed from the Sierras de la Ventana. Though not many remain, there are enough of them to give an idea of their well-bodied makeup. The language is special, somewhat like Tehuelche but a lot sweeter. The men are more handsome and taller than Araucanian men and the young women have nice features. When they speak they do so in a much paused, sweet manner. In this sense they have a lot in common with Guaraní speakers. The name of a woman who gave me some information was "Canviefel," which has a pretty ring to it. Ostrich is "gaye," lion is "aimá," guanaco is "petchua," fox, "yeshg'lay," man, "pastray," woman, "yankanke," etc.

I've made notes on the traditions and superstitions of these Indians. Near here there is a stone cave shaped by the relentless waters of the Río Negro when it was much farther above sea level. The Indians call it "Elengassen's Cave." Elengassen is an armored creature that stole women. The Indians say it looked like a glyptodont. According to others he was a very tall man who shouted loudly and blew in such a way that he always caused storms to break out around the cave. Any Indian who dared to pass nearby would surely fall into his hands and be killed by the monster.

For this reason the Tehuelches have carved out a convoluted path over the hill a league away from the cave in order to avoid passing by there. I have seen the cave and picked up some stone samples from it.

The "Ultralalve" is another monster. The Mapuches say he is half ram, half human. *Fire comes out of his mouth and eyes, and he is always mounted on a sheep. I was told by an Indian that there is one such monster around here that yells very loudly. When they speak of him, they do so with fear. Another "cuco" is the dreaded "Anchimallegen," but he is such a formidable creature that they refuse to even talk about him. All I know is that he is huge and shaped like a human.*

I'll be taking notes of these peculiar superstitions during my trip.

I've met an Indian here who is the illegitimate child of Coronel Hernández of Rosas' era. This individual has wed five times already. Four of his wives are dead and the two current ones await the same fate. One of them is dying of a stab wound close to the heart, a love-pat from her husband! These people are so simple they don't have feelings for one another. His other wife told me yesterday that Hernández was very wrong in paying the doctor five thousand pesos for his wife's first treatment. She reasoned he could have bought two better-looking ones for that money!

This same Indian has been good to me and he's given me a letter for Shaihueque's brother. He and Cacique Sinchel told me not to be concerned at all, that no harm would come to me. At worst, they said, Shaihueque might not let me cross over to Chile. In any case I will be able to see the mouth of the Río Negro.

If you don't hear from me by March or April, it probably means I haven't been able to cross the Andes into Chile and that I am making my way back.

Anyway, I will be in Buenos Aires for San Pascasio's.

I'm setting out again early tomorrow morning. When I get to Balcheta, Choele-Choel or Chichinal, and if I run into Indians heading to Patagonia on business, I will write to you. Otherwise I won't until I reach Chile. I'm healthy and happy, and I'm sure everything will turn out fine. It will only get boring during the three days of my first parliament.

I'll write soon and at length about this when I get to Chile. Bernal will send my broken watch with Rubado. Manuel Cruzado will send you a trunk load as well. It's for my museum. There are also two live foxes I've left in his care. Give them to Don Sebastián

Casares on my behalf. Write to me in Valdivia and don't worry. I'm less at risk here than you are there.

If you see Juan María Gutiérrez tell him that the language of the pampas does exist. It's no myth.

Farewell old man. Have faith. You'll soon hear from me in Chile.

Your son,

FRANCISCO P. MORENO

Letter Number 8

LETTER TO HIS FATHER

_____

Primera Angostura, December 6, 1875 (4:40 p.m.)

My Dear Old Man:

  I'll be leaving for Chile any time now. There are more than 100 men in our party. They are going to stop in Chichinal to wait for the Indians that stole the band of mares in Romero Grande. I will keep going. When I get to that spot, 120 leagues from here near the place where the Río Limay and the Río Neuquén converge into the Río Negro, I'll write to you all. You will hear from me in a month and a half or two.
  I wrote to all of you yesterday.
  I'm in high spirits. Farewell to all,

F. P. MORENO

_____

Note on the back – 62 years later!

Bariloche-Buenos Aires. Departure: 7 A.M. Arrival: 1:02 P.M.

  Memento of the trip made on the same date and to the same remote spot sixty-two years later, aboard an airplane from Aeroposta, Argentina. Covering the same distance in about six hours, it was the first passenger plane to fly over the area traversed by the heroic "Perito" Francisco P. Moreno in 1875.

"Patagonia Airplane."

December 6, 1937[22]

_____

[22] The Argentine writer Manuel Mujica Láinez wrote this text.

PART II

Second Expedition to the Cordillera
The Continental Divide
Return to Lake Nahuel Huapi
As a Prisoner of Cacique Shaihueque
in the Caleufú Camp
The Escape
1879/1880

PREPARING FOR THE SECOND EXPEDITION TO NAHUEL HUAPI

Patagones, August 11, 1878

Mr. Francisco P. Moreno,
Buenos Aires

Dear Pancho:

I'm writing by ground mail, since the post is leaving today. I'm pleased to inform you that I've made arrangements for your overland journey, following the instructions in your letter. I didn't send word via steamship, because the Indians didn't arrive until after it set sail. Now that they're here, I can send you this letter.

The Indians in your party are completely trustworthy. One is the son of the friendly cacique Inacayal; the other is Gavino. You've met both of them at home. I've made plans to give Inacayal's son one hundred cows and forty to Gavino, with an additional bonus of ten more cows as an incentive for him to bring you back in one piece.

Gavino's family is here but he doesn't want to take them with him. Therefore, in addition to what I just said, I've offered to provide his family with a monthly supply of 25 pounds of mate tea, 25 pounds of sugar, 25 pounds of rice and 50 pounds of bread while he is gone.

Half the animals promised in exchange for your protection will be furnished at the outset. The other half will be given once you return or once proof is received that you have made it to Chile, that you have remained there without incident, and that you are being taken care of as agreed.

Inacayal Jr. and Gavino must accompany you as far as you request, except for the crossing into Chile. They won't commit to that crossing unless they obtain consent from the chiefs in the area. You know who I'm talking about, Seihueque and Nancucheo. If those caciques allow you to cross over into Chile, Inacayal Jr. and Gavino will provide you with their most trustworthy men to accompany you to Chile's Christian territory. Once you are there, you'll send me the proof we've discussed before. If you don't cross over into Chile, Inacayal Jr., Gavino and their party will escort you back here.

If you buy the animals here, the cost is between 180 and 200 pesos for each one you give the Indians. Each horse is 400 pesos. Take these prices into account when you submit your budget for the trip. Don't forget to add in the supplies and the presents that are traditionally given to them.

Inacayal's son is in town, requesting the annual rations for his father in accordance with the treaty signed by his grandfather Huincabal, a friendly Indian, and the government. This arrangement has been in place for quite some time and its beneficiaries have never caused this town any grief. In fact there have been no complaints about their behavior. Huincabal's son, Inacayal Sr., is usually the one who picks up the rations.

The rations owed to Huincabal's people include 300 cows they were supposed to have received last year, plus this year's animals, supplies and clothes. They came and requested their rations, but have been told that there is no government order for the transfer of these goods. They have asked me to write to you and have you try your best to resolve the situation. If you did you would win Inacayal's support. He would then be more amenable to the government and would accompany you, which would ensure that you'd get what you want.

You could put forth the argument that upon his return from the journey, Inacayal's son, (his name is actually Vtrac), will enter into a treaty with the government, pursuant to which he'll settle near this town and engage in agriculture. He could bring people to settle the southern bank of the river.

It would be in your best interest to obtain the rations due to the Indians. Without them they will be unhappy and cause problems during your journey. They won't take proper care of you. Seihueque's and Nauncucheo's rations are equally important. The misinformation that Linares's people are trying to spread about you will put your life in danger if these Indians don't get their rations. Even if their rations are suspended once you return, if you please them now, you'll succeed in seeing what you couldn't see on your last trip. I hope to hear from you at the earliest opportunity as to what's happening with your trip and the rations of the friendly cacique Inacayal (or more accurately said, those of Inacayal Sr.'s father). Inacayal Jr. is waiting for your answer, so don't delay. I wouldn't want him to leave for the countryside without you. I've told him he may have to wait up to one month, but it would be better if you had an answer beforehand.

I'll send the quillango furs by steamship, along with whatever else you'd like. That's all for now. Best regards from your friend who is eager to help you,

MANUEL CRUZADO

PRELIMINARY ACCOUNT OF THE SECOND EXPEDITION TO THE CORDILLERA

Information about the Andes range and its environs was notoriously scarce. Time and again, mention was made of the need to back up our claim against Chile with precise geographic information. I had published some documents on the Chilean-Argentine boundary dispute , which established a legally justifiable border in keeping with our interests. As a next step I referred some people to a book[23] in print that I had authored. I took the opportunity to suggest the need for a meticulous exploration of the region and of the coastal areas of Patagonia and Tierra del Fuego.

It didn't take more than a few days for my wish to come true. I got official word that the national government welcomed an "exploration of the shores bathed by the Atlantic Ocean." I had been designated "to direct that important mission." That same day I wrote to the provincial government of Buenos Aires requesting a temporary leave of absence from my duties at the Anthropological Museum so that I could accept this assignment.

The leave was granted and I accepted the honorable commission on April 1. I offered my services without requesting remuneration. I did insist, however, that any items gathered during the exploration should be donated to the museum if found to be relevant to its mission. The national government granted my request, declaring that the country "thanks Doctor Moreno for the selfless patriotism with which he has set out to perform the difficult tasks inherent to his commission." (Article dated March 1879).

I immediately proceeded to organize the expedition,

---

[23] The book to which Moreno is referring is *Un Viaje a la Patagonia Austral.* ("A Trip to Southern Patagonia") printed at "Tipografía a Vapor," San Martín 208 (La Nación).

which soon enough met with difficulties. As often happens, low-level officials were countering the decisions made by their superiors. We were provided with extremely meager supplies. This led me to believe that not everyone in government wanted the scope of the expedition to reflect the breadth of vision of President Avellaneda and Secretaries Laspiur and Montes de Oca.

I was commissioned to study the situation at the Chubut colony. I was also entrusted with identifying lands suitable for settlement in the area between the Río Negro and the Río Deseado. Another task was to indicate a point along the Río Santa Cruz that offered good settlement possibilities and to procure a section of territory for that purpose within the law. I was also to search for nitrate deposits, whose presence was often alluded to, and study population conditions south of Río Negro all the way to Cabo de Hornos.

In order to explore the coasts, I requested a Navy ship equipped for the task, pursuant to the provisions of the above-mentioned governmental decree. This request, however, only made matters worse. At first it was alleged that there was no such ship available, though shortly thereafter the "Paraná" battleship was designated to transport the expedition. Use of the "Paraná" would be subject to the decisions of its commander, in accordance with the special instructions he would receive. From the outset these instructions undermined the very essence of our work as an exploratory commission. The "Paraná" expedition was diverted towards a military-scientific objective, while the part to be played by my commission was doomed to failure.

Under pressure to compromise, I settled for a steam-powered river cruiser, the "Vigilante," which had been on river patrol for the Navy and had the capacity for a 100-ton load. She had a five-foot draft and no keel. This vessel was clearly inadequate for a scientific expedition whose theatre of operations would span from the port of Buenos Aires to the dangerous Cabo de Hornos region. Yet I did not object to the official decision. The power and resources required for an expedition of this magnitude were in the hands of others. The decision-makers were enormously ignorant of conditions at sea and in the coastal and inland regions we would be exploring. I really had no choice. They were so indifferent when it came to risking the lives of others! Proof of what I'm saying can be found in my files. I reluctantly accepted the "Vigilante." One high-level Navy official predicted it would become my coffin shortly after I set out to sea.

Preparations for the "Vigilante's" expedition continued. Meanwhile, I distributed copies of my book, *Viaje a la Patagonia Austral*. It was discussed in the national Congress and deemed to provide valuable insights regarding the southern regions. When the government honored me by ordering a number of copies, I thought my troubles would soon fade away, but I was wrong. The commission was ordered to sail on the "Vigilante" and depart immediately. I barely managed to have an iron bulkhead built in the bow. That created additional space for the crew and somewhat mitigated the dangers posed by the raging currents sure to be encountered.

In early October, I was ready to start working so we set sail. We had received few supplies but an abundant set of instructions –most of which would have been impossible to follow. I don't think a single marine would have thought it possible for the "Vigilante" to navigate the South Atlantic successfully, much less the coastal waters south of the Strait of Magellan.

THE CONTINENTAL DIVIDE
AT NAHUEL HUAPI LAKE AGAIN

After a long hard journey, we arrived at the mouth of the Río Negro and voyaged through its waters for four hundred kilometers. This proved that the river was navigable up to that point, at least during that time of year.[24]

I braced for the task ahead, approximately a two-year stint in Patagonia, during which we would study the mainland and its coastál regions. It would be impossible for us to transport our work from the south to the north. We had no coal and no supplies to get us to Tierra del Fuego. We also needed to test the seaworthiness of the "Vigilante" while we were still hugging the coast. Once we ventured out into the hostile seas off the southern shore, there would be no possible rescue.

The first area to be explored was the territory between the Atlantic, the Andes, the Río Negro and the Río Chubut. One member of my team, together with officials from the "Vigilante," would examine the coastline and perform an in-depth study to determine whether the "Puerto de San Antonio" could become a major port connecting the Atlantic with southern Chile. As such, it would foster the settlement of the Argentine interior and the Limay-Neuquén triangle, through which I had passed in 1875-1876. This done, the group would go on to evaluate San José Bay and Golfo Nuevo, passing along the Valdéz peninsula coastline and Río Chubut, where it would meet up with the other half of the expedition.

I set the date of November 11 for departure from Viedma. An engineer, Francisco Bovio, would accompany me. I brought along two sailors, and two Indians –an Araucanian and a Valdivian. The latter had been arrested on suspicion of

---

[24] Letter from the President, Lieutenant General Julio A. Roca (See Appendix).

murder. In exchange for his freedom, he had promised to serve as our guide in these remote areas, through which no traveler had ever journeyed.

We had enough horses and plenty of mares to keep us nourished. Only Musters* had reached this area before. As the reader may recall, on a previous trip I had managed to sail the Río Negro. The much-commented Río Negro has been the scene of so many projects and so many failures. It could well become one of the most important passageways in the Argentine landscape. Yet government neglect and the selfishness of local landowners could just as easily shatter such hopes.

Many a thinking person who has traveled through the area is shocked by the inconsistency of government policy towards the Río Negro and the nearby San Blas Bay. There is abundant water for irrigation and a wealth of resources in these southern lands. Yet all sorts of resources for the development and defense of the southern territories are concentrated in the hands of a few. In spite of the grandiose projects, the wasted millions, and the tons of ink spent in describing and praising the region, the only thing to be found today is a small canal, a green plain, and a few hectares of fruit orchards.[25] Nothing more has been done in these lands, similar in quality to colossally productive areas in California and other parts of the Western United States! Scottish and English pioneers have been settling the region by the great river near El Carmen for the last fifty years. Yet they have attracted few others. Those who persevered can be counted on the fingers of one hand.

It would have been easy for those who controlled the national purse strings to fund an initial study of the region. It would have made all the difference in the world because it would have laid the groundwork for the national government to turn the Limay-Neuquén enclave into one of the

---

* Translator's Note: A reference to George Chatworth Musters.
[25] Written between the years 1917 and 1918.

wealthiest Argentine provinces. As a cohesive economic and geographic unit, its borders could have been easy to draw.

Six years after my first visit, I arrived to see few accomplishments in the way of progress. The Indian threat was gone, however, thanks to the westward expansion of the frontier from Bahía Blanca and Carhué to Choele-Choel. It was General Roca who achieved this goal, initially through implementing Rosas's plan. He then adopted Sarmiento's approach, which followed the U.S. model: combining arms of war with arms of peace and science. In this way, precise knowledge was gathered on soil conditions, so that the lands could be immediately exploited. Luckily for Roca, people listened. Once he earned their trust and the cooperation of his collaborators, he could move ahead with his plan, as there was no shortage of resources at his disposal.

The campaign itself seemed easy in comparison to the more difficult task of having to explain its remarkable significance. There were fewer Indians than might be suggested by their repeated advances, often separated by large distances. To be sure, "civilized" accomplices in the dirty deals and border intrigues were in abundant supply. The Indians were hardly able to put up a resistance. I am sure that thousands of lives could have been spared. Needless to say, many more "Indians" than "Christians" were killed.

The true story has yet to be written, a truly dispassionate and straightforward account that seeks out the facts about the struggle against the so-called savages. Although different from the western quest as it evolved in the United States, or against the _Araucanos_ in Chile, or wars fought elsewhere against people of other ethnic characteristics, there were certain heroic feats well worth remembering. Yet many people who fought to defend lands they thought were their own against the encroachment of civilization, were slain unnecessarily in the course of the struggle.

It is indeed true that a large number of villages and _estancias_ on the frontier were laid to waste by the savages. Yet how many Indian elders, women, and children were deci-

mated when troops stormed their encampments! The soldiers, obeying and correctly or incorrectly interpreting the
orders or gestures of their superiors, slit their victims'
throats, shot them dead, or tied them to stakes in the ground
and tortured them to death.

I have strived to pay due respect to the experienced young
officer, the hardy soul who risked his life defending the fort
every day, as well as to certain commanders who were truly
fair-minded and patriotic. Yet the book I am writing is a true
account of what happened, and I must say that I am among
the few who have accurately described our frontier wars.
There is a woeful scarcity of historians who can rightfully say
that they have penned a fair account of this fifty-year conflict.
Quite a few significant historical events have been left out.
Luckily, these omissions include some actions that violate the
tenets of Christian civilization. As for the ignorant nomads,
they fell prey to temptation and the lure of the unknown.
Christians, on the other hand, have no such excuse for their
actions. Neither can they claim that they acted out of revenge.
Their assaults upon ragtag Indian militias rooted out the
"rabble" by force. Indeed, there were a hundred times more
Indians who succumbed to the saber and the rifle than there
were soldiers and settlers who were felled by Indian lances
and *boleadoras*.* Moreover, methods were readily available to
subdue the Indians peacefully if they refused to be stripped
of their possessions or resorted to violence. It is common
knowledge that it was frequently the frontier traders who
incited the Indians to steal so as to seize their loot. They did
not care about the burning and killing that would ensue.
These and other similar matters were the topic of conversation that morning aboard the "Vigilante" with those who had
been nice enough to come and bid us farewell.

The small ship was scheduled to depart towards San
Antonio Bay as soon as we mounted our horses. An on-site

---

* Translator's Note: A *boleadora* consists of three stones tied together with a
rope, which is hurled at its target.

study would be conducted of the bay, the future transcontinental trading center from which goods would be imported and exported. It was lunchtime and someone noticed that thirteen of us were partaking in the meal. If we had taken this fateful number seriously, Bovio or I would have lost our seat at the table. It may seem trivial but the reader will judge later on the value of coincidences such as this one.

A few hours after our departure we could still make out the solid outline of the Patagones Fort tower looming up in the distance. Soon enough, we lost sight of the upright poplars and the leafy walnut trees. As we got farther from the coast and the islands with their verdant vineyards, we advanced deep into wetlands and silt beds, vestiges of the ever-changing river, for the valley was not yet fully mature. We traversed salt marshes, rocky areas, and dunes interspersed with lush meadows. The landscape was an uneven succession of flood-ravaged or drought-ridden areas. Nonetheless, I am confident that these desolate conditions will be overcome once an intelligent effort is made to uncover the vast riches that lie dormant in these lands.

I contemplated the extinct races buried in these areas, along with those soon to be extinct. Others would take their place and their destiny would be different. That led me to reflect upon ways to kindle a spark of patriotism among our anemic statesmen, who are generally apathetic unless working for their own immediate political gain. These so-called leaders refused to see that good crops grow when you plow the land. The plow was the only weapon needed to take over the valley, a valley that, as Sarmiento had noted, could benefit millions once the land surveys were completed. What a shame that the lands were sold for a mere pittance to a handful of well-connected do-nothings! The only contribution made by this chosen few was to delay the country's growth, which, if not for them, would most certainly have occurred. It was so hard to get the politicians to set aside their aspirations and steadfastly work for the future of the country.

I remained lost in thought until a stupefied Indian pulled

me out of my trance. Galloping past me at full speed, he held on to his demijohn full of rum and spurred his poor horse until it bled from the needle nails piercing its flanks. He was eager to get back to the orgies at the Indian camps. Over the green bulrushes, the slender reeds, and the white plumes of the pampas grass, the sky was suddenly filled with thousands of ducks, herons, and partridges. We were probably close to a streambed, as the soil was rich in hummus. Finally, it was nightfall, time to rest in a soft, fresh bed of clover, abundant enough to feed our horses. We would be hard-pressed to find food for them later on as we made our way through the desolate, thorny mesas.

At dawn the next day we woke up to the view of a newly established *estancia* and a few small farms. This was the work of true "pioneers," [sic] the most confident and daring dwellers of the open range, much more so than the "squatters" [sic] of the U.S. or Australia. In those countries, the law makes it easy for those who till the soil to take possession of it. In Argentina, these pioneers have often lost their lives or those of their loved ones in the process of defending these lands. Many perished as their ranches were burnt down and their cattle was stolen. Some say they should count their lucky stars for being allowed to stay on as mere "settlers" when somebody else gets title to the property. Fair or not, the fortunate new owner finds it easy to break the law by acquiring the land on condition that he will settle it, and then does so by using these pre-existing pioneers as his "settlers."

All in all, a different landscape has begun to emerge. The red brick of the farmers' houses is back, dotting the wheat fields with a splash of color. Gone are the remnants of the San Javier Indian encampment, where idleness and witchcraft became even more entrenched upon contact with white men. This type of backwardness, formerly seen in and around frontier towns, severely held back progress on our frontlines. A new breed of man developed in these remote regions. He acquired bad habits; got involved with the criminals who had found refuge amid the decadence of the Indian camps, and became as calculating and lazy as the Indian himself. Dealing with these people, I've noticed they have no self-respect. They are full of envy and can be treacherous with both Indians and whites. Indeed, they seek to dominate Indians by feigning submission and hatred for Christians. In Indian raids and sneak attacks on frontier villages it was their meanness and viciousness that caused the most havoc, but it was the Indian chiefs who were ultimately blamed.

The following can serve as an example of how devoid the mestizos are of humanity. We were passing a sheep pen made of thorny branches. To one side, on a pile of manure surrounded by skeletal remains there was an Indian who had terrible sunburn and looked ill. I approached, but he wouldn't talk. I asked people in the next tent what was wrong with this ailing man and why no one was coming to his aid. I was told that a friend of his had been shooting at the moon one night to scare away evil spirits. In the midst of such madness, the injured man was hit in the head. The people with whom I consulted carried him to the corral because his boss, a mestizo, didn't want anyone dying inside his house. This poor man hadn't eaten in three days. Left to fend for himself against the elements, he had endured the last rain as his high fever devoured him.

I examined the wound; it wasn't serious. The bullet hadn't fractured the skull; it had just pierced the scalp. However, having been left there to die, the poor soul didn't stand a chance. A small incision with a scalpel and a good cleansing were enough to make him react. Fortunately, there was an empty wagon headed for El Carmen, so I asked the wagon driver to take him there. Shortly thereafter, however, I learned that he had been left to die in the same spot where I had found him.

That Indian, who hailed from the Andean foothills, had been traveling through the area hoping to sell guanaco skins and furs from his hunt that year. He met his fate among the mestizos. News of his death reached his nomad tribe far away, filtered through a dark veil of mistrust, and provoked strong passions, since Indians attribute bad deeds to Christians. I've seen Indians abandon sick people in their villages as well. It seems only natural when there is no known cure. However, when white men act in this way, the Indians curse them because the assumption is that the white man doesn't want to find a cure.

In the course of my involvement with Indian affairs, I have met up with the following argument on the part of the Indians: "Why don't Christians take care of Indians as they take care of their own? Why do they despise us? Christians complain about us capturing women and children, but we don't kill them as they do our people."

The way the Indians see it, the land is theirs and white man has encroached upon it, so they must get even. Nevertheless, their brutality is no match for our own. Indians follow certain time-honored rituals. In their "parliaments" they always remember their ancestors, who were executed en masse by the forces of the tyrannical Rosas. They also vividly recall the government's "Desert Campaign," dating back less than twenty years, in which executions were almost a daily occurrence. Our beloved country thus lost thousands of her native sons, useful hands when properly overseen! Even as we speak, those who view the natives without bias can see that the remaining few have more good than bad in them.

Two days later we arrived at Guardia Mitre. Located nearby is a vast plain with great agricultural potential. An Indian caravan was camped out there. They were Mapuches, "apple-growers." They knew about my plan to reach the Cordillera south of Nahuel Huapi and had reservations about it. Sinchel, the old cacique, lived there. He was one of the last Pampas or Gennakens. Once rich and powerful, when I met him again, he was almost destitute. Sinchel remembered Captain Musters, with whom he had been friends. I had met Sinchel six years earlier, during more prosperous times. Although he had endured adversity, his misfortunes had not soured his character. He was still a pleasant and caring man. His tall figure, his reddish-brown complexion, and a demeanor reminiscent of a redskin chief made him stand out among the other Indians as a quintessential survivor of a dying race. Wrapped in his big guanaco fur, he performed the usual ceremonials with as much courtesy and self-assuredness as any civilized man. He recognized the superiority of white men over aborigines and was aware of the fateful destiny the latter had in store. He told me I would be welcome at the many Gennaken camps along the way. Those territories, he told me, belonged to his grandparents, and it was no use dwelling on the settlement possibilities they offered because Indians were lazy and ignorant but white man was all knowing and he would make good use of the land. He said that evil spirits had prevented these Indians from learning to work. This character flaw made them different from the Pampas Indians of Buenos Aires.

While in this area I explored a small natural cave the river had carved into the ravine's tertiary formations. Sinchel told me a story borne out by other Indian elders' testimony about the time when the cave served as a shelter where Elengassen, a strange, huge creature, used to live. This was before part of the cave crumbled, reducing its dimensions. Some say Elengassen was covered by an enormous, thick shell, very similar to that of an armadillo. He was probably a glyptodont. He stole women and had a human face. Others describe him as a gigantic person with armor plating on his back, his abdomen being the only vulnerable part of his body. The Indians said he would burst out screaming and puffing so hard that he would create a fierce, never-ending storm around his lair. Whoever dared to approach the monster's den would be promptly exterminated. People were so afraid that they stopped using the path along the riverbank and adopted another, one league away. Not everyone agreed that the monster had ferocious tendencies, though. Some Indians argued that he wasn't destructive and that he never captured anyone, but they admitted he hurled stones at whoever got too close to his lair at night.

What everyone agreed upon was that at one point it became necessary to choose a new path. They seemed to remember a time when their land was free from the monster's presence, although the explanations were quite varied. The women, who often used the trail alongside the river, said that they feared the creature because he threw stones at them and let out "hideous growls." The men rarely took that path on their hunting expeditions.

I explored the remnants of the cave and found traces of the type of art Tehuelche women painted on quillango furs. The bottom of the cavern was covered with iron-bearing rock, so abundant in these tertiary ravines, which in some spots was bluish-purple in hue.

Hernandez, a Gennaken mestizo, lived there. He claimed his father had been an officer in the Argentine army, and there was a good chance this might be true. His companion was another mestizo of the same ethnicity, one of whose ancestors had reportedly formed part of the Fitz Roy expedition. Hernández was surrounded by all the comforts any civilized man could desire, but hadn't completely given up the ways of the desert. Shortly before I arrived, in one of his frequent drinking bouts, he had stabbed one of the two women who shared his bed because she was "annoying." Later he regretted the whole thing, so he decided to have her checked by a doctor. The doctor charged approximately five hundred pesos. His other woman, Carmen, complained bitterly and said it would be wasteful to heal this woman when two prettier, more available females, could be purchased for the quoted price. Hernández was immediately persuaded. Shortly thereafter, when the Indian woman died of her stab wounds, he promptly married the survivor in a traditional Catholic ceremony. I talked him into coming with me on the trip. Five years earlier, he had accompanied my friend Jorge Claráz, the reputable geologist, on his overland crossing from Río Negro to Chubut. Now I would be able to count on someone who was familiar with Gennaken customs and practices and had maternal relatives scattered about in the areas I was planning to visit.

Luckily, another long-time acquaintance of mine, Gavino, born of a Gennaken mother and a Mapuche father, agreed to come along too, even though he was not in good health. When I showed up at his tent, he was cheerless. He had dreamt that I had gone to the camps without him, to which he took great offense.

The friendly overtures of these Indians made me realize how easy it would have been to set up a commission made up of good Indians with strong ties to the Indian camps of the Andes. Using their influence, those tribes would have surely accepted the control of the national government. Rather than heeding my arguments, made public since 1875, the Remington prevailed and caused the annihilation of thousands of people who could have led productive lives.

Shortly after we left, we came across an encampment of Indians who told us they had come from the foothills of Neuquén and were there to trade hides, feathers, and hand-woven fabrics. It seemed odd to us that they would stand their spears in a row on the ground, since we knew it was forbidden to carry them across the frontlines. I had a feeling we were up against more than just a bunch of traders. This region was populated by a small number of Indians living under submission, and there was no reason to fear the presence of horse thieves. Yet, I noticed that their horses were heavily guarded, which implied a readiness to fight and gave credence to my suspicions. Before long, I had become convinced that I was right.

We made it to the last Christian settlement. Some Basque pioneers lived in this spot, their golden wheat fields thriving in the rich soil inhabited today by prosperous people. There we struck up a conversation with another contingent of Indians from the Andes unknown to either Gavino or Hernández. They were Chilean Indians, *"borogas,"* who rarely ventured as far as the Río Negro. They were moody, underhanded, and, unlike the true Mapuche, lacking in social graces. They tried to alarm us, averring they were peaceful people, and that it was the Andean tribes that were plotting to revolt. I found that hard to believe, however, as I had just heard the news about nine wagon drivers murdered in the Chichinal area.

Three years earlier, I had had a run-in with some Indians at the very site of their demise. The Indians had raided the province of Buenos Aires after the great invasion of 1875. They were on their way to sell their loot to the Chileans. What I heard merely confirmed my impression that behind the veneer of trade, these *borogas* were preparing to move against valley settlements. What's more, the site where the victims' bodies had been found also yielded a few slings and hand-woven fabrics of the kind used by the Picunches from the Andean valleys. Great numbers of these Indians were among the presumed traders. I could not but rush to Choele-Choel to alert the villagers.

Bovio remained behind to take charge of the caravan. Further ahead I arrived in Conesa, a small developing town. There, the same mistake made on countless previous occasions was being repeated: allowing recently surrendered Indians to crowd into the new town centers, where farming was more necessary than cattle-ranching. Instead of setting up reservations like in the United States, the government let Indians live like gypsies. The Indians set up campsites wherever they pleased, and nothing whatsoever was done to turn them into useful tillers of the soil. I'd see them lying in the sun enjoying a smoke and basking in the warmth while their women picked lice off their heads. They were too lazy to provide for themselves now that the government provided them with a ration of meat, sugar, mate leaves, and other conveniences while they idled away their time, their minds free from worry.

I arrived in Choele-Choel, the main army base, strategically located at the same site selected for that very purpose by Rosas during his 1833 Desert Campaign. Currently an agricultural center, it is destined to become a cornerstone upon which this new nation shall be built. When I talked to General Villegas, we both agreed there was something afoot and that the murderers of Lopez' troopers were hiding among the armed Indians I had encountered. I returned to the Castro camp with two seasoned veterans inured to the dangers of the backcountry and with a military unit that would imprison the Indians. We left Castro and continued our march. There were sixteen of us, some Indian, some white. Eleven of us thought we had enough weapons, but when the need arose to use the Remington cartridges from the batch I had obtained in Buenos Aires, they turned out to be useless.

In the cover of night we climbed up the bleak, desolate mesa. We had no water. The next day we crossed the Gualicho lowlands, one of many basins cutting through Patagonia. Their origin is still being debated. These depressions appear to have been formed when sedimentary layers broke off and the soil was laid bare, a phenomenon I attribute to volcanic eruptions, very modern in relative terms. They have taken place on a large scale in the area. Subsequently, a detailed study was made of this region, when plans were being made for a canal that would divert water from the Río Negro to Puerto San Antonio. Nonetheless, the issue of these depressions will not be resolved until we have a true geographic map of the coastal and central Patagonia area. At the center of this low-lying land, whose elevation is below that of sea level, rain and snow form a small stream during the winter months that dries up later on when the air is warm, leaving a trail of white salt in its wake. A great number of marine fossils are found in the adjacent canyons. There we found a cave similar to the Elengassen cave. The Gennaken Indians call these vestiges Ayaguay-Huag, while the Araucanians refer to them as Epehuén-Geyú. Inside the cave we saw other remains of the past: cave paintings, empty bottles, pieces of cloth, a horse's mane, cigar butts, and scraps of newspaper offered by superstitious Indians in the belief that the Good Spirit would protect them against mortal thirst if by misfortune they were to lose their horses.

As we marched further south, the rocky surface of the mesa became even bumpier. It was covered in part by pebble stones; some of which were moderate in size and prevented the growth of small bushes: *chañares* trees *(Geoffroea Decorticans)*, the resinous *jarrilla (Larrea)* bushes, the trailing carob plant, the *mata negra (Brachyclados Lycioides)*, *palo de sebo (Monttea Aphylla)*, as well as tiger's claw plant, the characteristic flora of the sub-Andean region of Argentina.

We noticed that several small lakes containing sodium chloride were surrounded by exuberant shrubbery and abundant grass, which signaled to us the presence of fresh water slightly beneath the surface. This was later proven to be the case. Present-day herds thrive in this formerly desolate mesa.

As we advanced deeper into the southwest, soil conditions improved, making the land more suitable for the pursuit of human endeavors. We came to the sizeable Valcheta Lake. It is located in the same general area as Walichu, but has far better economic potential. When we arrived on the 29th at noon, we cooled off in a clear stream that emptied into a small gorge whose sides were picturesque granite rock formations.

The region's geography unfolded as follows: The semi-arid northern mesas gave way to rocky hills. Looming in the distance to the south, we sighted perpendicular shapes of black volcanic massifs, quite a change from the landscape we thought was characteristic of Patagonia, the "land of mesas." Scattered about near our campsite we found petrified tree-trunks measuring up to one meter in diameter and fossilized marine mollusks from the early tertiary period.

We had cut across the Indian trail that stretches from the Limay past Huincul Mapu, a country broken by low hills called the great lowlands of Mackinchau. Once the trail reaches the Valcheta Valley, it climbs up the mesa to Castro, along the Río Negro, and on towards the sea along the El Chancho track near Carmen de Patagones. This is the same *Camino del Chancho* trail followed by Musters with the Tehuelches in 1871.

To the north lay the vast saltpans that cover the low country, where the stream sometimes flows, and the high volcanic plateaus with their blackened volcanic cones rising off the grassy valley. The Gennakens called this land of promise by the stream Yazuepash-Malash. It was here that the Castro and Chancho trails converged on their way to the Río Negro, as did the Aguallá and Pajalla paths used by the Tehuelches and Gennakenes to get to Chubut. The only source of fresh water and relatively abundant grass is located at this junction. In my mind, these favorable physical and geographic conditions destined Valcheta to be the closest strategic point, economically and militarily, to San Antonio Port, approximately one hundred kilometers away. I spent two days studying the area, as my instructions were to search for sites with such characteristics between the sea and the Andes.

The negotiations I subsequently undertook were based upon impressions gathered during this trip, along with the results of studies conducted by the "Vigilante" in the Bay of San Antonio. I was able to get the government to lift a ban on the sale of land adjacent to the port area. Then I took measures to ensure congressional approval of a plan to advance railway construction so that the Atlantic and the Pacific would be linked via the San Antonio and the Valdivia corridor. There was an urgent need to deepen our knowledge of this central area, given the uncertain situation in Argentina at the time and the threat to our national unity. A comprehensive study would still be extremely beneficial today. Thirty-five years later, we do not have a map of the region located between Río Negro and Chubut, at least not one of which I am aware or that is worth mentioning. All we have are some rudimentary sketches. As far as I can tell, no serious geological study has been conducted of the area. Indeed, land surveyors' maps contain infamous errors that have cleared the way for the sale of Patagonian territory at a loss for the government. As my story unfolds I will have to revisit this issue time and again.

This was a pleasant, restful time for both my men and my horses. My museum collection also reaped some benefit, as evidenced by the gathering of burned human bone fragments, abundant arrow heads, primitive mortars of the kind used by indigenous people to chop up guanaco jerky, and fresh water mollusks probably used by Pampas Indians to eat with in times past. We continued heading southwest until we

passed a lake now called Lake Chanquin, its beautiful emer-
ald green waters surrounded by shiny yellow, red, and black
rocks, granite and basalt formations from the tertiary period.
We made our way up the broken ground of the mesa until
we spotted the high volcanic peaks of the San Antonio sierra
to the south and the soaring Semoncura Mountain tapering
into small grassy valleys watered by brooks, all of which
flowed in the direction of the enormous Valcheta basin. Most
of them later emptied into salt-water lagoons. We could see
an elevated mountain range above the mesa level far in the
distance to the northwest. This was the remarkable Huincul-
Mapu region, which means "the Highlands" in Araucanian.
Unmapped at the time, it used to be a desolate area, but it is
now well on its way to becoming a prosperous cattle-ranching region. We saw the first craters that once spewed out
black lava. At this point better soil conditions render the land
fit for exploitation. Water is more abundant, there is more
pastureland, and the areas are better sheltered. The terrain is
a lot more rugged further northwest, southwest and south.
To the southeast, one can see high mountains. Gone are the
broad, flat expanses so typical of the Atlantic region.

On December 6 we left the gorges and gulches behind and
crossed great volcanic massifs towering more than a thousand meters high. We took Jagagtoo's pass. The small craters
looked like they had just erupted, their volcanic scoria a fresh
mantle of red and yellow. A look inside, though, revealed a
grassy core sprinkled with calceolaria (a South American
plant), a sign that the sleeping giant had been dormant for
some time. The rolling hills of lava had deep cracks, exposing
black basalt walls that plunged down from them. We followed a broken trail of mesas, some rose up, others were
sunken or on a slope. Still others were separated by deep
gorges whose cracks had not suffered the effects of erosion.
As we came out of this maze, through the majestic gateways
and archways that bridge this amazing geological site, we
advanced into the vast plain of Yamnagoo, an area lauded by
the Indians. The broken mesas, culminating in steep basalt

ridges like the remnants of fortresses with wide irregular gulches looked as if they had been carved by Cyclops.

We camped out at the Sheela springs next to a huge wall –another richly textured geological landmark– looming large over us and casting shadows over the lake and rushes. Light flooded the rocky plains, which reached towards the sunlit contours of a faraway mountain range. We hadn't encountered any Indians yet. All the Indian camps had been abandoned so we stopped to give ourselves time to think while our horses rested. As impressed as we were with our observations of the ever-changing landscape, our experience would have been more complete had these spectacular vistas included the presence of man. A mantle of gloom hung over the area as I searched in vain for the nomad, whose colorful presence would have livened up the lackluster solitude of the desert.

We journeyed through stunning vistas, past shady ravines, mesas, vast shrub-covered plains, rushing streams, and large red rocks of irregular shapes resembling the denuded remnants of mythical sphinxes rising among the grasses. Giant clusters of basalt were reflected in the surface of the water in the lagoon, and mirages evoked magical images. We discovered that we were not too keen on the eerie silence of the desert, broken up at times by a guanaco's neighs or a condor's caws emanating from the mist that hovered over the deep gorges all day long. As we left the populated areas farther and farther behind, our safety became less of a concern so we were glad to see thick columns of smoke rising up in every direction around us, announcing that Indian hunters were in the immediate vicinity.

The smoke rings were huge, but in the middle the plain was deserted. It seemed that death had stalked the camp dwellers. A few steps from the site where we pitched our tents we found several slaughtered horses that my guides recognized as having belonged to an old witch doctor who had recently died. Further along, near the vestiges of a new Indian encampment, there were other dead horses that had been hung by the neck. The Gennakens, who inhabited this forsaken place, as well as the rest of the Patagonian tribes, customarily drown the horses of their dead to prevent blood-letting and thus ensure their future use in the after-life. That afternoon we found the medicine man's tomb in the adjoin-ing mesa. The cane that held the sacrificial mare's heart was still in place, having been left there to keep death out of the region. The funerary cairn was made up of huge chunks of basalt rock. It was the same type of tombstone I have often found in my travels through Patagonia.

The Sheela (meaning "Reed") or Yamnagoo basin mea-sures one thousand square kilometers. Ages ago it was cov-ered by water, evidence of which can be found in the dense alluvial deposits abundant in gravel. Large rocks were scat-tered about. They had broken off from other rocks that, according to my guides, could only be found "in situ," in the mountains along the southwestern boundary of the region. There's no doubt in my mind that this movement has been caused in part by advancing glaciers. Indeed, the terrain merely has a gentle slope. It is a long haul, and the edges of the rocks show no signs of erosion. The Appá Mountain Range borders the southeastern edge of the plain. To the south, the Dalaguepu Sierra looks just like its counterpart. Indigenous people pass between both ranges on their way to the Chubut River. They have told me that it is beautiful coun-try down there and that water is abundant. The Guichakell plains, home to Chief Chiquichano's tribe, are covered with pastures, making the area a hunter's paradise, the Indians said. Currently occupied by a good number of squatters who have taken it over, this neglected region ought to be studied before being parceled out and sold. Careful planning must precede the subdivision so that it doesn't compromise efforts to develop the Central Patagonian Territory. Sadly, this part of our land is just as unmapped as when I visited it back in 1879.

Lying before the Dalaguepu massif were tertiary volcanic mesas. Smoke from hunters' campfires could be seen rising from the valleys. Large basalt walls rose to the west, east, and north of us, ranging from one hundred to one hundred and fifty meters high.

On the first day our attempts at making contact got no response, so we proceeded to send two messengers in search of inhabited camps; one went south, the other northwest. Meanwhile, we hunted guanacos* in Yamnagoo, a stretch of land in Patagonia best known for its game herds. However, before we could enter the hunting grounds, we had to obtain the landowner's consent.

It was indicated to us that the landowner was a large irregular rock fragment that represents an elderly woman whom the Indians believe to be the owner of the neighboring lands. This large rock was covered with objects given by hunters as tax payments and consisting of branches and poncho scraps. We also contributed a generous tribute at this altar to the primitive history of rock worship.

The hunting grounds border a salt-water lagoon fed by a fresh water spring. This is the best drinking water in the vast area surrounding the lake, with the exception of the camp itself. All the guanacos in the region come here to drink. On a hot day these animals line up in droves to get to the fountain. As they approach, their view is obstructed by the small brown hills that line the edge of the lake. The guanacos are unable to see what's happening on the other side of the hill. That's where the hunters hide. Whenever the thirsty troop of guanacos line up, the hunters pounce upon them at full speed, always with bountiful results. Given the abundance of game, the fact that this is the sole source of potable water, and the advantages of the surrounding terrain, even the least skillful Indian on the worst horse is able to make a catch. He knows for sure that he will find food in Yamnagoo, so this place is sacred to him. The payment of tribute to the woman/rock is a superstitious reaction to the fear of catching no prey.

---

* Translator's note: *Guanacos* are relatives of the llama.

The stones neatly arranged in front of the lake in the vicinity of the hill validate the assumption that religious forces dominated the Indians' outlook at this junction. The stones are laid out in semicircles comprised of huge lava fragments, forming an arch that faces east. Measuring no more than fifty centimeters in height, some of these stones have already been destroyed. They are covered with a large quantity of skulls, long bones, and vertebrae from dead animals. The path to the fountain is lined with three rows of animal skulls. In one of the rows I found more than 200 skulls methodically lined up one after the other. This age-old custom goes back farther than my Indian guides could remember, and I should say it proves how grateful Indian worshippers were to the Good Spirit for procuring them game animals. As much as they liked to eat the head of the animal, they left it for the Good Spirit.

It was a fine day for us. We were rewarded with several guanacos, ostriches, and *quirquinchos*,* which allowed my guides to show off their knowledge of Gennaken cuisine. We were getting tired of eating the old worn-out mares that had been our sole source of food. By now, they were hardly a pleasure. Therefore, we replaced them with guanaco, ostrich stew, and quirquincho barbecued over hot rocks, among other foods.

We all feasted on the new foods, but the good cheer did not last long. The two messengers came back without finding any Indians at all. The rain set in; one of my men rolled over on his horse, and another man's best horse suffered a broken leg, the warning signs of a string of misfortunes coming our way. One of my Indian companions dreamt that a serpent entered his body, a matter not to be taken lightly, as it pointed to his wife's infidelity. However, the most ominous sign, a harbinger of future calamities, was when one of my guides felt his eye quiver. The Indians in our caravan, that is to say eight out of the sixteen men in our party, were deeply affected by this, and

---

* Translator's Note: The *quirquincho* is a mammal resembling the armadillo.

the gaiety came to an abrupt halt. I think the main reason for the change in mood, even though they didn't say so out loud, was that we were approaching the area sometimes traversed by Araucanian enemy tribes. In addition to this threat, our Indian companions were worried about rumors they had heard in Río Negro upon our departure, which predicted that our journey would come to a bad end.

To prevent the cloud of mistrust from being further spread by idle talk, we cut our rest short and resumed our travels on the 11th. We crossed a volcanic region through torrents of basalt rocks, crystal-bearing tufa, and tertiary formations sometimes covered by a layer of ancient glacial debris. We passed by a red oxide deposit that Indians use to make paint. We then trekked across a hill that juts out from a fresh water lake. This is an avian paradise from which we could see the most fertile land we had encountered thus far on our journey.

This jagged landscape shaped by crevices encompasses a mix of exuberant valleys and somber ravines of relatively great beauty. Our view was probably enhanced by the presence of large herds of horses, in the middle of which stood a large number of white mares.

We realized there must be Indians in the vicinity, since they are never too far from their herds. The presence of a few cows and a small flock of shaggy-haired sheep was a sure sign that the encampment must lie hidden just a few hundred meters off.

We broke into groups and climbed the last hill, bracing for an encounter –friendly or unfriendly– with Gennakens or Araucanians. Moments later we were at the summit.

Down below in a narrow green valley, amid numerous hot springs surmounted by volcanic massifs that resemble huge ancient ruins, were the wretched tents. The panorama was filled with domestic animals and a few women carrying firewood or water pouches on their way from the fountains. Followed by their sniffing dogs, a group of young men crowded around the hunt they had caught with their slings that morning.

All was quiet at the campsite. There was nothing that gave away our impending arrival until the cowbells hanging from the necks of our animals started clanking as they descended the steep mountain. That put everyone on alert. All of a sudden the men who had been sleeping in the sun ran every which way in search of their horses and spears. The old women, who are the certain victims of wars among the savages, hid in the thick shrubbery. The young women gathered on top of a small hill to ponder over their future in the hands of a possible new owner. The poor Indians had no clue what to expect. They ran their horses up and down trying to round up the herd, but didn't seem to be in a hurry to come closer to us. Eventually they approached, yelling at us and asking if we were their friends. My guides recognized them and introductions ensued. Shortly thereafter we were surrounded by forty half-naked men who stared blankly at us.

Through the interpreter we learned that we were among friends here at Cacique Puitchualao's. He was chief of the Gennakens. For years I had been waiting for the chance to meet these people. The men were still wary but the youth joined us, and the young women aged 12 to 15 mingled with my men, who piqued their curiosity. They were barely clad, though some were wrapped in dirty fur blankets. When they saw us lighting matches they were so smitten that they forgot their initial apprehensiveness.

I pitched my tent a few meters from my new friends' campsite, which took up an eight-meter area. The moment we had been anxiously awaiting had arrived. We were about to experience life in the wilderness in the beginning stages of civilized society.

We set up our tent. The Indians' fears were put to rest following the shock of watching us handle the theodolite, a measuring instrument that gave way to a lively discussion among our simple-minded observers. At that point, we noticed all eyes were fixed on us. The old women came out of hiding and one by one began to march solemnly until they were face to face with us. They circled around us in single-file and broke into song, a cacophonous melody accompanied by hundreds of howling dogs of every imaginable type. At times the chorus was interrupted by a series of never-ending chants, "ahua-lá hue-lé, ahuá-lá hue-ló, ahua-lá huelehuel," uttered by the haggard sixty-something crowd. As the young people and able-bodied men continued to examine us carefully, comfortably resting on their gentle horses, the women performed the welcoming ceremony of the children of the desert. It was not only a gesture of respect towards our guides and their families, but a musical celebration in remembrance of their brave acts. Like the Red Skins in North America, the Gennakens had distinguishing family emblems. Our caravan was led by descendants of the once powerful "days" or "marching sun" family, represented at present by a very small group of individuals.

There was something utterly repulsive about the old hags, their wrinkled skin the color of old oak daubed with red and black paint, their beady eyes squinting behind a filthy mop of stiff, greasy hair that added to their disheveled look, their drooping breasts covered by a dirty blanket thrown over their protruding bellies. Their smell was unbearable, but they didn't seem to notice. As the grand celebration continued, their awful smell filled the air around us. They waited for a gesture of generosity from the white intruders. We finally granted this in the form of mate and sugar.

Although we were no more than 100 meters from Puitchualao's hut, we had to send a messenger to announce that I was on my way to greet him. My host had laid out his best furs and cushions for the occasion. I sat there with my great companion Bovio, the engineer, and flanked by our two guides. The Chief's two daughters were in charge of piling up as many furs as possible behind us so we could rest our backs after a long and tiring journey. Puitchualao was sixty or so. His square face was covered with wrinkles, under which one could get a glimpse of the solid construction of his skull. His long hair was held back by an Araucanian headband, and his body wrapped in a new quillango fur that allowed one to see his broad brown chest, along with his robust arms and legs. When he shook hands with us, he had the air of a civilized man. He introduced us to his older brother, "Captain Chivo," who claimed to be known far and wide. He indulged in a long speech delivered in the indigenous language of the Pampas, the essence of which was explained to us through an interpreter. He had never dreamt that he would one day be able to offer us his hospitality.

When it was my turn to speak, I told him I had heard about the feats of valor of the Pampas Indians, and that this had bred in me a strong desire to meet them. As a token of my friendship I offered him a demijohn of *aguardiente* liquor (after generously watering it down) so they could celebrate the encounter. The gift was cordially received with numerous signs of appreciation and vigorous handshaking. Captain Chivo said he thought we would have heard of him in our country. Showing us his hand he said, "it's silver," alluding perhaps to his purported good fortune as a hunter.

You can't be too squeamish if you are going to spend any amount of time at a Gennaken camp. It would be difficult to describe how filthy the place was, and I have already talked about a similar one, the "kau" of the Tehuelches, elsewhere. Suffice it to say that the two young women, the prettiest females the Pampa Indians had to offer, the ones who were crouching next to us with cushions for our backs, spent their time effortlessly swatting flies by slapping each other's flesh and munching on these insects while they discussed the white visitors they had never seen before, their glasses, and their strange ways. As they chatted, the women partook of a snack consisting of bits of lamb fat that they shared with two grumbling bald men.

Fortunately Puitchualao's thank-you speech was brief. Had it been any longer, we would have had to put off drinking. Usually, among Patagonian tribes, a good speech will last several hours or even days. Puitchualao said tragedy had struck his family. Two males and two females had died, which caused sorrow and grief that our presence helped alleviate. Joy once again filled his heart, in evidence of which he extended his right hand to us once again. Immediately thereafter he took two spears, drove them into the ground, and sprayed *aguardiente* over them as he appealed to the Good Spirit to grant protection to the white men who spread good will throughout the land and its local inhabitants.

The whole gathering, ourselves included, promptly joined in the act, asking for an abundant hunt of guanacos and ostriches, and for fewer riding accidents. During the invocation the women kept singing their monotonous songs.

Even though the *aguardiente* was exceedingly watered down, everybody in the tribe got drunk that night and it was impossible to sleep. The young women rolled about in the spring water and the old ladies were pulling out their own hair, moaning loudly about their past misfortunes. Meanwhile the men kept picking fights. Puitchualao spent the night trying to find me in order to demonstrate the great friendship he felt towards me. The next morning found him lying at the entrance to my tent where he slept all day long. As if I hadn't noticed the state he was in, on the third day, he sent word that he had been drunk for two days. It was his way of pleasing me by letting me know that he and his people were doing well.

These people belong to an American tribal group on the brink of extinction. They are doomed, like the brave Charrúas from Santa Fe province. Ten years from now there won't be a single one left from among the populous group that once met the Spanish conquistadors. The decline of certain American races is proof of their inferiority vis-à-vis other indigenous groups of America who can resist the pressures of the encroaching white civilization much longer except when their destruction is accelerated by the force of arms. The Gennakens, as well as the Ahonekenes or Patagonians, are destined to disappear from the face of the earth soon. Their downright primitive customs cannot resist a rapid change of environment, and they shall languish and perish without being able to assimilate with the invading races.

Civilization has not taken root among these people. The Patagonian tribes are not like the Araucanians, who want to become useful to society. I know of no Patagonian or Gennaken Indian who has been able to overcome his or her inherent laziness, and in this sense, Patagonians are inferior. What goes on among these races is notorious. They don't oppose the arrival of civilization, yet they do not accept it. When they settle down temporarily to life in the village, they sometimes appear to be more developed, but as soon as they go back to the desert, they return to their nomadic ways. With the exception of a few utensils and weapons given to them by white men, these two races are still in the Stone Age, in the prehistoric ages of the world. If they have given up the arrow, it is because they have horses and dogs, which, together with their *bolas*, suffice for hunting. If no iron knives are available they will fashion some with gravel. I have seen how they skin *guanacos* with these primitive tools. One can see the methods of times past in the way they prepare their quillango furs. There are thirteen operations necessary for making a well-made robe, and not a single European instrument is used in any of them. All that is needed are a few rocks to rub animal skins down, sand, fat, natural paints, quartz, obsidian rock to make scrapers, bone needles, along with ostrich tendons that are spun and used as thread. It would simplify the job to use metal tools, but indigenous women won't have anything to do with them. They often laughed at me when I repaired my old cloak using a thick mattress needle and cotton thread.

The presence of the Gennakens and Ahonekens in the Southern territories is comparatively recent. Indeed, they have replaced other racial groups, which died out hundreds of years ago, (as is shown by the remnants on exhibit at the Anthropological Museum.) The two groups resemble one another greatly, although there are differences between them. Gennaken skin is darker and Gennakens are shorter, but both groups share many physical features: a broad, square face with a severe but pleasant look, almond shaped eyes, lips that don't protrude much, a nose that's not too flat and can be aquiline. The Gennakens have higher cheekbones. Because of the big difference in height, Gennakens have smaller faces, smoother features, and their bone structure is less rough in the area of the skull. Both groups are very muscular, have broad chests and small hands and feet. They both share the same customs and limited economic development. Some Gennaken women weave, but they have learned the craft from the Araucanians, who probably copied it from the Peruvians. They have no knowledge of pottery, even though prehistoric groups did.

The Gennakens' very existence has been shrouded in mystery for a long time. I think I was the first one to call them by their real name when I made my first trip to Nahuel Huapi Lake in 1875 and 1876.

In 1829, however, they were studied by Alcides D'Orbigny in Carmen de Patagones. Musters offers scant information about them. A distinguished Swiss geologist, Doctor George Claráz, also examined them, but his conclusions have not yet been published. Some have gone as far as denying the Gennakens' very existence and have lumped them together with other Pampas Indians, failing to take into account the great differences noted by D'Orbigny. I believe there is an explanation for this. First of all, their numbers are small and they've always lived far from civilization. Secondly, D'Orbigny has given them a generic name, Puelches, which basically means Eastern peoples. Araucanians and other Andean tribes (Aucas) call everyone who lives in the plains to the east by that same name.

The various tribes that make up the Araucanian race have always been confused and their names have sometimes been misinterpreted. References are often made to Puelches, Mamuelches, Ranqueles or Ranquelches, Mapuches, Pehuenches, Moluches, Aucaches, Hiliches, etc. Sometimes they are considered to belong to various groupings when in fact they are one and the same race. They take on different names according to the various areas where they live, so much so that a Puelche coming from the east can become a Huiliche (southern people) if he moves south. The Mamuelches (forest people), and the Ranqueles ("*Carriales*" people), have regionally-based names, but are considered Puelches by those who live further west. As for the Puelches, they consider the people who live on either side of the Andean foothills to be Moluches. Actually, the Moluches inhabit the Chilean foothills, while the Puelches occupy the Argentine base of the mountain. To the inhabitants of the Nahuel Huapi area, the tribes who used to camp out in Neuquén are Picunches (northern people).

Each tribe, however, calls itself by a separate name in relationship to the open range. Gennaken means people from the Pampas or plains. They call Patagonian Indians "Isnaken," that is to say, southern people, or inhabitants of the south. Thirdly, Gennakens have been identified with the word Pampa, a Spanish translation, which in Buenos Aires is used in reference to the indigenous tribes who live in the Pampas, namely the Araucanian races. This confusion has gone on for so long that no weight is given to D'Orbigny's opinion. He believed the Puelches (the Gennaken) were the Querandíes who used to live in the area now known as Buenos Aires. I tend to side with the wise French historian, and one of these days I will seek to prove him right.

It is generally accepted among the Gennaken that they formerly inhabited the plains of Buenos Aires. The elders like to remind me of the time when they lived in the sierras north of Tandil. They migrated south a century ago. In D'Orbigny's times they occupied the area between 39 and 40 degrees latitude, mainly located along the banks of the Río Colorado. Originally a very large group, wars and disease had reduced its number to roughly 500 or 600 individuals. These days I've seen them 300 kilometers south of the Río Colorado. I don't think I'm exaggerating when I say that there are no more than 20 true Gennakens living in Patagonia. Their migratory history can be traced by looking at the funerary remains scattered along the route they followed. I have often said that the Gennaken are physically similar in appearance to the Patagonians, but they speak a completely different language especially from that of the Araucanians. The Gennaken have a tendency to change the names of words considered unlucky, such as the names of people who have died. This practice makes it difficult to compile a precise dictionary of the language as it is spoken. I have made similar observations with respect to Patagonians and Araucanians. Unfortunately, I cannot provide much information about the Pampa language. I was unable to finish my research due to the sudden and almost tragic way in which my trip ended.

The Gennaken have not only suffered losses due to war and disease. Combat provoked by the Gennakens themselves has also contributed to their demise. It is known that the tribes inhabiting Patagonia don't understand the concept of death due to disease, much less what causes disease. They attribute this mystery to witchcraft that, they believe, was employed against the patient by an enemy. They take the advice of a witch-surgeon, who always has some adversary against whom he holds a grudge. That person is blamed as the cause of the problem and is condemned to face the enmity of the sick person's family. If that family is rich and powerful and the alleged culprit is poor, then he or she is doomed to ruin and is sentenced to pay with livestock, game, or silver garments. If the patient dies, the culprit is destined to suffer the same fate. However, sometimes both families have powerful relatives and friends, in which case war is the only answer. First there is a confrontation between families. Then the confrontation expands into a tribal skirmish. My guides have pointed out several battlefields where they once found themselves either fighting on the same or opposing sides. These Pampas have seen great medicine men among the Patagonians and Araucanians. The Araucanians in particular have unleashed bloody campaigns with numerous victims. I heard about an old woman, a powerful witch who on more than one occasion predicted an attack. Initially, her words fell on deaf ears, so, when the offensive was launched against the Gennaken camp, it resulted in its complete destruction.

These wars of revenge are true acts of carnage. Everyone is lanced to death or decapitated: men, women, or children. Not even domestic animals are spared. I met an Indian who was the sole survivor of a whole tribe exterminated in this manner. Sad to say, superstitions are so deeply ingrained in these people, they will only die off when the people themselves disappear.

We reached an out-of-the-way valley called Yaguelcaguay ("House of Parrots). It was small, hemmed in by volcanic rocks and obviously glacial in part. The enormous irregular black crystals of the lava formations resemble huge black gothic towers. They loomed large over the humble fur tents. Despite its rich soil, the area was bleak. Fed by spring water, vegetation covered the basalt lava floor, but the accumulation of glacial gravel moraines made it impossible for anything but thorny bushes –cactus– to grow. The basalt is red and black with lots of streaks in certain parts. The campsite is located at 41°51' latitude south and 70°16' longitude west of Paris. It lies 992 meters above sea-level. As such, it is higher than the Andean region to the west. (According to my observations, the altitude in Nahuel Huapi was only 723 meters.)

On December 13, I notified Puitchalao that I would soon be on my way again. The goodbyes lasted two hours. Puitchalao was not very articulate but, since he wanted to make a good impression as a speaker, he recounted the many times he had lit the fire in his hut, how he had kept it going, the troubles the women went through to find firewood, and the great benefits provided by the hearth, especially in winter. It all reminded me of the primitive practice of fire-worship, which forms the foundation for the world's great religions.

Captain Chivo also showed off his prowess by rendering an account of his imaginary battles, and asked me to tell everyone he was in good health. We packed up camp quite early and struck out towards the Andes. The old women renewed their monotonous chanting and the young ones picked up the empty sardine crates prized by Indians for their value as dressing tables. These poor people live in abject poverty. Their laziness and filth make it impossible for them to live more comfortably. When travelers leave these campsites behind, they feel as if they had come up for air. As frustrating as it is to be alone in the desert, no humans in sight for weeks, one soon tires of this indigenous society. Yet it is not so much repulsion as pity that one experiences at the sight of these wretched populations.

Moments later, we lost sight of good old Pitchualao's encampment. We were almost certain that we would be the last travelers to see the Gennaken people and witness their nomadic lifestyle.

Just a few days' distance meant a world of difference. Thousands of years separated us in social terms bringing us back from the Stone Age into modern civilization. The Yaguelcaguay camp and its environs will probably be the last stage in the life of this Pampa race, which three hundred years ago put up a tenacious resistance to the founders of Buenos Aires. Their demise will not be brought about by weapons, but by the fatal influence of a superior way of life. These tribes will disappear from the face of the earth, concluding their modest evolution after having reached the level they deserve on the human scale. All they leave behind are a few bones and stone scrapers, the last vestiges of human life from the quaternary period. Despite all the transformations that progress has brought, these remnants have persisted from the infancy of human development.

It will be hard to imagine, a few years from now, that these remote areas were home to a whole race that died off there. It will be hard to believe that the strewn broken rocks are all that's left from a way of life that dates back to the depths of the previous geologic era and came to an end without undergoing any change whatsoever.

Much has been said about travelers' weariness but nothing about the rewards that await them. I doubt there is greater compensation than being able to see with one's own eyes the entire range of man's physical and moral evolution. In looking back upon things past, from the rural huts of yore and the fauna that has been lost to the modern metropolis, one marvels at the process of evolution.

Museums and libraries preserve a part of human life in the form of material objects. Yet the infancy of mankind's social life, the origins of man's intellectual life and the psychological manifestations thereof can only be found in the wild.

During my travels, my spirit has often tapped into images of early man and those of his civilized descendant. I derive great intellectual satisfaction from such reflection, but my pen cannot begin to describe it.

Despite the higher elevation and increasingly uneven terrain, conditions in general improved substantially as we went on. At times we had difficulty walking because the exuberant grasses often hid streams underfoot. Guanacos abounded and were restless. Condors appeared by the hundreds over the lava beds, silently flying in circles up in the sky, a sure indication that several Indian hunters were in the vicinity.

We crossed mountainous country and set up camp at "Yamerua Yamgue-Gchaul," which in the language of the Gennaken means "where there are *vizcachas** from the sierra."

We found ourselves at the foot of an isolated mountain of solidified lava. It was the region most likely to be settled, possibly towards the western side of Valcheta. It generally runs from the southeast to the northwest. The landscape to the north is nothing but a succession of mesas characteristic to the area. The southwest is mountainous land that seems to run parallel to the one previously mentioned. There are a few volcanic cones in between the two. We saw an abundance of rocks that are not only foreign to the region, but also whose size, condition, and distribution bear out my theory that glacial phenomena are involved here.

Yaulonuka-Tage (meaning, "the place where roots are cut

---

* Translator's note: a South American rodent hunted for its meat.

off") is an area where certain edible plants grow, which could very well be consumed in lieu of asparagus, if only people were willing to try them. It seems like the ideal setting for an *estancia*; several in fact could prosper in the region and its environs. Many small caves or caverns can be found there. Carved into the rock where the lava meets the sand, they date back to the tertiary period. We also saw paintings like the ones previously mentioned, as well as guanaco and ostrich bone fragments that look like they were once used in Indian cooking. In addition to these we collected carved flint stones and a young man's skull cap, cut in half in order to be used as a makeshift plate. When I reached this spot I left part of the caravan there with Bovio and then headed north towards the famous Mackinchau plain Musters had visited in the past.

I had already told the Araucanians at the Río Negro and those I met at Puitchalao's campsite that I'd be taking the Mackinchau trail to get to Limay. It was my understanding that they would so inform the tribes in Neuquén.

This plain is another centrally located region that would be quite suitable for the establishment of permanent communities. It currently belongs to the British Southern Lands Company (*Compañía Inglesa de Tierras del Sud*). The national government sold it with blatant disregard for its economic and strategic value. A study was finally conducted by the Commission for Hydroelectric Studies for purposes of designing and laying the railroad to Nahuel Huapi. However, the study was limited to the area traversed by the railroad and its immediate vicinity. The remaining area is just as topographically and cartographically unknown as when I visited it years back.

The Indians told me there were similar lands abounding in salt water lagoons and fresh water further to the west and northwest. Further to the northwest, they stated, water flowed towards the Río Limay. Nonetheless, due to the absence of guanacos and given the smoke we observed over the trail that leads to the camps further west, I decided not to head along that path. I had a funny feeling the Mapuches were planning a sneak attack, as I later confirmed. I returned to the campsite, trekking across lands that were relatively poor in resources and unsuitable for herd keeping. The floor is granite-based volcanic rock.

Bovio was waiting for me in Maictk, at the foot of a mountain range formed by granite rock, so far the highest mountain range we had found. He had explored the caves where, according to my guides, their ancestors had lived. Then it was my turn to do so, and I was able to ascertain that they were indeed natural caves or caverns, some deeper than others, which were formed in the basalt rocks so prevalent at the foot of the mountain. The site had been well chosen by the Indians. It was abundant in game and its streams and lakes were teeming with fish. The area was hidden from view and afforded lookout areas, diminishing the likelihood of an ambush. Some of these caverns had served as living areas, kitchens, etc., and others as gravesites. The biggest one was 8 meters wide by 30 meters deep, and had a height of 12 to 15 meters in front.

I believe that excavating in that cave would yield results of the same caliber as the discoveries made at the Mylodon cave in the Seno de la Última Esperanza (Gulf of Last Hope). A small cleft in a nearby rock caught my eye. After clearing the way, by no means an easy task, I found a large quantity of human remains, as well as a few skeletons with their spines still attached. Mixed in with them were thin pieces of coligüe and cohigue* painted red and used as sticks for small huts, thin broken pieces of coligüe, some reeds used to make cradles or arrow shafts –the tips of which were sometimes made of flint or obsidian stone– as well as scrapers. Everything seemed to suggest that this out-of-the-way spot had been inhabited by Indians before. I concluded that the dead had been buried with all their household goods. The sticks had been used to attach stretched hides that served as the sim-

---

* Translator's Note: Branches used for thatching.

plest of shelters from the wind, rain, and snow, as witnessed by the first seamen who reached the Patagonian coasts. I retrieved twelve skulls, some of which were painted red, and a good number of skeletal remains, not to mention several mollusk shell fragments and a hand-woven remnant made from coarse guanaco wool. I made similar discoveries in a nearby cave, and noticed that the children had been buried in small openings, separate from the adults.

Another large cave surpassed all of the rest in size and could have easily fit fifty people on horseback. It had volcanic rock walls adorned with painted shapes, red, yellow and white, resembling those seen on fur blankets or *quillangos*. The floor of the cave, where I found a myriad of ostrich bone and guanaco skull fragments, all of them very old, seemed to have been artificially shaped in the form of an inverted dome. Upon excavation, we encountered a woman's skull and some arrow heads at a depth of one meter.

I would have liked to spend more time examining this veritable village in a cave. I call it a "village," as the population, given the rich hunting resources, appeared to have been relatively stable. However, since I only had two soldiers at my command, I had to keep going. Bovio had remained with the Indians at a safe distance. That way, he could keep them from becoming suspicious of the research I was conducting in these caverns, which were so mysterious for them. According to their ancestors, these caves were home to evil spirits, huge monsters whose powerful breath caused the heavy winds in the basalt gorge. The Elengassen cave is somewhat different. Speaking of this subject, it would be worthwhile to analyze the muddled recollection some Patagonian tribes have of the great mammals that are now extinct.

Upon returning from these excavations, I found two Indians from Cacique Kual's camp. They filled me in on the latest news from the backcountry. I learned that the western expansion of the frontier towards the Río Negro, had given the Picunches in the Cordillera good cause for alarm. They were starting to feel the effects of the shortage of livestock.

Accustomed to raiding the provinces of Buenos Aires, Córdoba, and San Luis, they were in for a reversal of fortune. The smooth-running operation in which live animals were casually exchanged for Chilean *aguardiente* was in trouble. I stuck to my plan and marched on towards the southwest lest Kual's Indians revealed my location to the Mapuches.

The landscape was typical of the area. Volcanic rock jutted out of sedimentary-rock mesas formed during the Tertiary period. As we moved farther and farther south, the lava fields disappeared in the distance. The presence of phenocryst and melaphyre became most prominent. Creeks running north or northwest were now as frequent and abundant as the grassland and wooded areas. This region was ripe for development. Here we discovered yet another large cave, which had formerly also been home to Elengassen, according to my guides. The walls of the cave were adorned with the same type of paintings as the caves I described above. The abundance of carved flint stone and broken bones suggested that it had been inhabited by ancient humans.

The volcanic range seemed to run northwest to southeast, although according to my guides, further south it ran east southeast. The range had high peaks covered with snow year-round. They were known as the Talagulpa Mountain Range. In the western foothills, in an Indian enclave they called Calgadept, I saw true moraines, which descended towards the east and southeast of a range that enclosed the valley on that side. At the base of the range lay the source of a stream that fed into the Río Chubut, cutting across a great plain where Cacique Chiquichano's tribes once lived.

The weather changed. One day it snowed heavily even though it was summer. Fortunately we were able to find shelter within the protective walls of the valley. Further ahead towards the northeast, the region was mountainous. Through the gorges we could make out the Andean peaks in the immediate vicinity of Lake Nahuel Huapi. In the far distance towards the west we saw other peaks draped with the white and blue colors of perennial snow.

According to Gavino, the Río Chubut ran south of a high basalt plateau. He said that he had once seen surging hot springs along the high mountain passes in the region and an abundance of a certain type of rock out of which his *boleadoras* were made: hematite. We also found a warm-water spring along the way, which gave off sulfuric steam. Located right next to a small lagoon, it served the Indians as a source of sodium chloride. In those areas, we found reeds taller than any we had seen before. They were undoubtedly used for making arrow shafts.

As we proceeded west past an older geologic formation made up of clayish mica, we found the first northeast tributary of the Río Chubut. We forded this river at an altitude of approximately 800 meters above sea level. The region's general features were changing: There were willows, a tree of hope in the semi-arid valleys, while the soil became increasingly sandy and filled with an abundance of glacial debris.

Once again we found traces of man in the form of a mule abandoned in the mud. Our Indian companions recognized it as belonging to a Tehuelche named "Ojo de Pulga," ("Flea's Eye"). There were no more volcanic rocks to be seen in this region, where the Patagonian mesa had reappeared with its boulders, pebbles, and occasional hunks of rock resembling the ones we had last seen west of Santa Cruz.

We headed up the mesa but before long we were descending towards another stream. We forded this small tributary and yet a third one. They both merged with the former and then emptied into the Chubut.

The next day we set up camp on the banks of a rushing river in a lush valley dominated by rugged mountains to the northwest. To the southwest, the foothills were covered with forests. Through a vast clearing in the central area and towards the west we could see the nearby Andes range. We were finally there! We had made it to a site that held the future of Patagonia in its hands. Once we had established a presence by populating this region, industrial development would follow and the basis for a legitimate claim to the southernmost portion of the continent would be firmly laid.

This area's reputation as an inhospitable place has caused a noticeable delay in its development. What's more, it has led to many arguments regarding its possession. Our trip was turning out to be as successful as I had hoped it would be. Without the joint effort of people and industry along the Patagonian coast, the central area and the Andean region, our claim to these lands and their wealth would never have been taken seriously.

Today, my vision has a foothold in reality. Those magnificent prairies are the site of numerous ranches. My dreams have come true. The area has grown in population, prosperity, and well-being. Today, this vast expanse is full of automobiles. How I long to go back to those places and see them in their present state.

There, among the rocks, I hid my collections. I was determined to come back for them when I headed back towards the Atlantic, along the bank of the Río Chubut, after completing my exploration out west.

The messengers I had sent to look for Cacique Inacayal's Indians returned from their mission. Utral, Inacayal's son, had lived with me in Buenos Aires. Word had spread in his camp that I was coming and that my intentions were hostile to the Indians. My old friend Shaihueque had already sent a party to the Mackinchau area with instructions to bring me to his camp. In addition, he was to be immediately notified of my exact whereabouts. My messengers also informed me that Inacayal and his companion, Cacique Foyel, had camped out three days south of our location. I decided to go and find them, though Gavino and Hernández did not like the idea. Gavino had once lost a son in the area. He also claimed that while he was sleeping the night before he felt one of his eyes move, which to him spelt imminent misfortune. Hernández said he had not only felt his foot move, but had dreamt he was being attacked by a wild bull, an unmistakable sign of impending death.

Skirting fertile valleys, we worked our way across the mountain towards the west, away from the large clearing where, according to my guides, the water flows westward through the snow-covered mountains, leaving big beautiful lakes in its wake. This region was once inhabited by the famous Chululos, an Indian tribe later exterminated by the Mapuches. Musters has recorded a good and accurate description of this leg of my journey, and I encourage my readers to read his account. Indeed, there is no point in replicating what others have described so accurately. My work, entitled *"Evidencia Argentina,"* also makes a detailed summary of a study conducted and published by the Hydrographic Studies Commission, which takes an in-depth look at the region.

In keeping with Indian custom, when we got to the first huts at Leleg, I notified Inacayal and Foyel of our arrival. We spent the night in another picturesque valley that crisscrosses the land. It is called Leppa Valley. There we celebrated Christmas in Patagonia for the third time.

We were struck by the beauty of the cows and bulls. In size and strength, they were unmatched by any we had seen in the Pampas of Buenos Aires. Everything pointed to the rich promise of the *estancias* that would one day grace the area. I was unabashedly optimistic about the future prospects of this land, and am happy to say that my predictions have been amply exceeded.

The next morning we ventured into a wide-open plain, the Esquel Pampa, where grass and water abound. Today, an *estancia* thrives in this very spot. The landscape became even more scenic. It was spotted with red clumps of strawberries that delighted our senses and uplifted our spirits.

We kept going and traversed another great lowland that extends to the west, eventually reaching the snow-capped peaks. There we had a chance to see another of the region's unique characteristics, namely rivers whose headwaters are on the eastern side of the Andean foothills and that flow across the mountain range to the Pacific Ocean. This physiographic phenomenon was of concern to me, because it was relevant to Chile's insistence that the dividing line be drawn at the watershed between the two oceans.

Halfway between Esquel and Tecka, we ran into Utrac and a few young men. Utrac had come to greet us on behalf of his father and Foyel, who were ready to see us. We traversed the great moraine that borders the area to the north. Late that afternoon we sighted the enclave of tents in the wide-open green meadow. The Argentine flag I had given Utrac several years before fluttered over Inacayal's hut, serving as testimony that the region and its inhabitants were all Argentine. Utrac asked us to wait awhile, so he could tell his father we were ready for the welcoming ceremony. He returned shortly with another group of young men armed with spears. On the end of his, he carried the Argentine flag. It was encouraging for us to be there on such a beautiful afternoon, our feet firmly planted on the fertile soil, and the blue and white national colors underscoring our determination to affirm our sovereignty over this region. For ever since the Lastarria proposal was drafted the Chileans had been seeking to take possession of these lands.

Despite the many obstacles encountered from the outset, my action plan was evolving successfully. The Indians wished to show us a sign of their joyfulness as well. Both Indian chiefs, who were very intelligent, understood that our arrival was a peace pledge. They wanted to express their delight in a manner consistent with the "customs of the people of the open range."[26] The welcoming ceremony began with a ritual called "circles of joy," in which we took part. Fourteen of us galloped in circles around a long line of 130 warriors. The deafening roar of their voices was nothing less than mortifying to our horses. When we made our third cir-

---

[26] Moreno returned the favors (See Appendix).

cle, the show of joy became more raucous. A well-built Tehuelche, almost naked and armed with a big *facón*, a colonial sword perhaps, took the lead as he stabbed the air, ridding it of evil spirits that might cause disharmony between locals and newcomers. Behind him, groups of young men lashed out at those same spirits by waving their lances in the air. Once we stopped racing around, we placed ourselves at a great distance from one another so that the circle would be the same size as before. Then Inacayal, Foyel, and their men started their rounds. Their enthusiasm clearly surpassed ours, as was seen by their shouting, firing of shotguns and rifles, and constant bustle of lances. Once the three laps were completed, as part of the same ceremony, I sent a messenger to make an announcement. He stood fifty meters from the Caciques and chieftains and said I was coming to shake hands with them –my right hand. There were fourteen of them as well, so we exchanged pledges of friendship twenty eight times, with some extra handshakes extended on their part.

"It is an honor for us to have you here, visiting from so far away. Yet surely there must be some other purpose for your trip, and so, I have gathered all my people so they can hear my friend speak." Those were Inacayal's words.

I said in reply, "Inacayal knows his son Utrac is not only my friend but also like a brother to me and has been so for a long time. He must also know that I had promised to visit him in his own home, just as he once came to mine, and I'm fulfilling this promise. In addition, my government has asked me to visit the Caciques living south of the great lake (Nahuel Huapi, that is) in order to find out what their needs are. I meant nothing wrong by coming here. On the contrary, seeing the national flag unfurled over the huts and protected by brave lances proved to me that the *paisanos* (the Indians) are the owners of the land, just as we are owners of the lands from which we have come. We are all Argentine, and we all have the same government in Buenos Aires." I added as an afterthought, "Some of you have been there and have been well received. I'm sure you can still remember where the seat of government is. Let me see, Utrac, where is my house?"

The nice young man immediately pointed in the right direction. Everybody became convinced that my intentions were good, though some of those present had lingering doubts about my true motives, especially the Pehuenche Cacique "Patria" and the Gennaken Cacique Puilchicaya, who considered themselves to be the region's legitimate owners. They insisted that my trip had another secret purpose. However, their suspicions were soon laid to rest when I sat down to talk to them in front of the main tent, alternating the conversation with gifts I knew they would appreciate.

I set up camp approximately twenty-five meters from Inacayal's hut. He and Foyel reciprocated the social graces by coming to visit us. We had a long talk, as they showed an avid interest in everything I had to say. They loved the passages I translated from the book in which Musters mentions them. They had so many questions that they stayed until midnight, at which time their visit came to an end. Before they left I answered their questions about the major stars, which shone so brightly in the pristine southern skies.

Although I was highly interested in examining these Indians, I could not stay in their camp any longer. It was imperative that I quickly move ahead with the actual purpose of my trip. Thus, the following day, I met with Utrac, by now my inseparable companion, Hernández, and Gavino at the big hut. Rumors about the murder of Lopez's troopers and word of the Mapuches' unrest had reached the encampment. We held another formal session. "My government," I said, "asked me to bring back information about the needs of the people in the rugged country, from the Río Negro to the tip of the earth, and for this reason I scouted

---

* Translator's note: Guides who know their way around the range.

out some *baquianos** to come with me to Nahuel Huapi and then return to Tecka."

My hosts decided to call a new council of the elders, because from their viewpoint, my plans to head north were dangerous. I would not only be exposing myself but also my Indian friends to Mapuche ambushes. One of these elders had already recommended to me in Leppa that I should go back the same way I had come. His advice was based on the broad range of experiences gained throughout his long life –he said he was one hundred thousand years old and had been imprisoned by Christians in Azul ten thousand years before. This didn't prevent him from treating me with a lot of respect, however. Indeed, he listened to my very convincing argument in favor of continuing my journey. Utrac supported my position. Foyel asked for a three or four hour delay to come to an agreement with Inacayal. An old chieftain who was one of Gavino's fathers-in-law would have sided with me on this point but couldn't, because his daughter was away at the time and direct contact with his son-in-law was forbidden. In Gennaken families, tradition mandates that the father-in-law never speak with the son-in-law, or the mother-in-law with the daughter-in-law.

On December 30, however, Inacayal sent word that he was ready to talk. Puilchicaya, who had come to believe he was the "national government," presided the meeting. Inacayal and Foyel usually lived farther north, though this time they had camped out temporarily in Tecka to be closer to guanacos, mesa ostriches, and wild cattle that roamed the western forests. Puilchicaya, who at the time was on bad terms with the Mapuches, considered himself to be a permanent inhabitant of the region. The rest of the Tehuelche and Gennaken chiefs, in his opinion, were transients.

The elders opposed my plan to travel to the lake. They knew I had been at the lakeshore a few years before and were concerned that Shaihueque might do something nasty when he learned that I was back again. In the end it was decided that Utrac would come with me. On the fifth , I sent a mes-

senger to Patagones. He was to give an account of the preliminary results of my trip.[27] I spent the next few days visiting Puilchicaya's tents and exploring the adjacent valleys, all
of which were suitable for permanent agricultural and farming communities. I also held conferences with the Indians
who were coming to greet me from all over. I met with
Tehuelches, Gennakens, and some Mapuches who had been
driven from the northern huts on account of family squab-
bles, tribal rivalries and bad spells, and had made this area
their home.

On January 8, we broke camp and resumed our journey,
leaving behind four men who were in poor health to guard
our luggage. When we got to Kashkell, I saw a beautiful row
of *fluenna*. We labored up the mountain range to the west,
along a trail leading to a region occupied by wild horses
described by Musters in his writings. I was determined to
find a path across the body of water that empties into the
Pacific, in order to get to Nahuel Huapi from the mountainous chain referred to as the *pre-cordillera* (the foothills of the
Andes). Exercising my right as first visitor to the area, I chose
to name it Rivadavia. I planned to return to Tecka through a
valley I had reason to believe lay between the actual Andes
range and the eastern *pre-cordillera*. It was a perilous journey.
We already knew that the party General Villegas sent out had
come upon four Indians who had managed to avoid capture.
They had made it safely to Shaihueque's huts with the alarming news.

We reached a wooded area, where trees grew among the
ancient historical markers we call glaciers. The foothills were
covered by erratic rock formations, and the gorges bordered
by moraines. We headed down towards the place we longed
to reach, the region whose waters flow west. At the Suenca
Pana Lake I saw the first stream. Its water ran smoothly over
a series of terraced steps, which in turn were remnants of a

[27] Report to Minister Zorrilla. (See Appendix).

vast ancient lake. The water flowed down to a valley that stretched before our eyes, but was rimmed by permanently snow-capped peaks to the west. Through the mountain gaps, the stream, now a river, would empty into the Pacific Ocean, Puilchicaya said. According to the Indians, further north in the same valley, another river ran north to south, then quickly turned towards the west and crossed the mountain range. Yet another river did so as well, but from South to North. That river had its source in a great southern lake by Puilchicaya's camp. Puilchicaya had told me about it.

It mattered tremendously to me to have found proof that several bodies of water cut across the Andes range, including Bío Bío River, which flowed from Lake Lacar, the Aisen and Huemules Rivers, and three others. Such a phenomenon is rarely seen in the hydrography of other countries, and neither our negotiators nor those from Chile were taking this phenomenon into account when drafting proposals that addressed the boundary issue.

Certain prominent jurists knew much about the ways of man but were ignorant about nature. They tried to interpret it without studying it, and developed their own concept of the continental divide along the mountain ranges. Little did I know at the time that I would be engaging in an endless battle, an exhausting struggle against the vain incompetents whose bad judgment clouded the issue.

In Esquel[28] we came upon Chief Huircao's camp. Huircao was a Mapuche and had bad news for us: Shaihueque had sent a search party to look for us. My good friend Bovio suddenly felt ill on account of a lingering ailment aggravated by the hardships of the journey. Despite his exceptional energy, he was unable to continue; we had to part ways temporarily. Bovio would return to Tecka where he would recover while he awaited my return. I would have to do without him for the

---

28 62 years later, this beautiful town would witness the birth of his great-granddaughter María Elvira Benítes Moreno.

time being. I continued my journey north with Utrac, our numbers cut in half. On the 11th, we passed through Quelu-jagitro and ventured into unfamiliar territory. The Chululak-enes used to live in these parts. It was beautiful country. To the west there was a great basin, which, according to my guides, was covered by a lake, the source of another river that cut across the Cordillera. Today this area is known as Cholila, a successful agricultural and cattle raising community. My trip would end not far from there in Caguel Huincul ("Hill Blocking the Way"), a breast-shaped volcanic protuberance sculpted by glaciers. It was in this Alpine setting that Utrac's family was camping out.

We felt it best to stay there for several reasons. Nonetheless, on the 16th, we got word that a hostile band of Mapuch-es was coming our way. Utrac tried to alert his father, so that he in turn could send people to help us defend ourselves. However, my good friend was unaware of the trouble his people were up against.

When we were gathered around the fire, Gavino opened up to me and spoke of his nomadic life. He mentioned mur-derers who poisoned people to death, saying that he had lost a son to one such assassin in that very spot. He warned me not to try any food the women might offer. I should have known better than to take his word lightly. One afternoon, shortly after we arrived at the huts, one of the women showed up in my tent carrying a pitcher of strawberry sap. Hernández and I ignored Gavino's warning and helped our-selves to the tasty dish offered to us, nudging away the hand of a poor little slave girl who belonged to Utrac's wife. In the early mornings, she had often come to my campfire to light a stick. We would always give her a little sugar and some other foodstuffs from our provisions. The young girl kept trying to stop me from eating out of the pitcher. I thought she simply wanted to eat the fruit herself. Finally, I let her take the pitch-er away. In the meantime, Hernández finished his portion, which was larger than mine. Hours later, he was the one most intensely affected by the toxicity. As for me, I medicated myself with laudanum. I was anxious and in pain all through the night. Despite my predicament, I offered to help my companion that morning, but he wouldn't listen to me and preferred to be cared for by an old sorceress who worked as a doctor. This local woman broke into song as she walked around the patient, making a rattling sound with a vessel full of pebbles she kept shaking in an effort to summon the good spirits. They would enter the ailing man's body and find out the cause of his malady. She touched his head and stomach and announced that he was starting to heal since her magic had scared the evil spirits off. Actually the treatment did nothing to keep poor Hernández's condition from worsening.

Dismayed, Utrac wasted no time in unveiling the truth about the poisoning. His woman had done this in a deliberate attempt to prevent us from leaving on our trip. She had learned that Utrac had another woman in Río Negro, and yet a third one in Nahuel Huapi. Fearing he would take on a fourth one when he visited Patagones again with me, she could think of no better way to stop him than to do away with Hernández, Gavino, and me.

As I headed north with Hernández, his poor condition soon deteriorated. Not long thereafter, I was forced to leave him at a hut along the way, where one of his relatives lived. He died there a month later, as the type of poison involved had a delayed but violent effect.

On the 17th, we quickly passed through Chief Royil's hostile territory. Luckily for us, the people in the huts had drunk themselves to exhaustion, but one of Shaihueque's messengers caught up with us. He had a letter from Loncochino, a half-Indian who had become "Secretary of the Superior Government of Don Valentín Shaihueque." Loncochino had previously served as some sort of secretary at a Catholic Mission in the province of Valdivia.[29] The letter invited me to visit the

---

29 See appendix for Cacique Shaihueque's letter.

great chief once again in Caleufú. It also stated that he wasn't plotting to capture me. Such rumors were unfounded. The armed men sent to Mackinchau, he said, were merely there to escort me on my journey and defend me if necessary. I was already familiar with the deceptiveness of the half-breeds. Yet I preferred to take my chances, rather than go back without first getting to know the topography to the south and west of Nahuel Huapi, a region known for its famed Bariloche pass. I would confront deception with cunning. As we moved north, we began to see a greater number of rugged hills to the west. Gently rolling hills, formed when volcanic rock forced its way up against the sedimentary layers, appeared like huge colorful belts that skirted the snow-capped Andean peaks.

On the 18th we left the Río Chubut basin and ventured out into the Limay basin. We forded the Río Pío, or Río de las Hechiceras. Finally, we reached the top of a green hilly area strewn with large glacial debris. From there we caught sight of Lake Nahuel Huapi's blue waters.

AS A PRISONER OF CACIQUE SHAIHUEQUE IN THE CALEUFÚ CAMP

On January 23, 1880, I discovered a new lake and named it after Dr. Juan María Gutierrez, whom I admired. Feeling quite happy with the way my day had turned out, I returned that afternoon to the same site where I had left my helpers. My collector's sack was heavy with many interesting geological fragments I had picked up. My backpack contained beautiful samples of the area's diverse vegetation, among them, cypresses, oak trees, fuchsias, and ferns, which bear witness to the richness of the soil. I relished the sight of the spectacular panorama before us, the romantic lakes, forests, and snow-covered summits that are the prominent features of the Andean landscape. I smiled to myself as I envisioned the future of this "Switzerland of America."

I was certain that the Bariloche[30] pass was ahead, and that we could use it as an escape route if the way south was blocked off, but I had forgotten to factor the menacing Indian presence. Any time now, the Indians would sneak up on us. My mind wandered as I made my way upwards to the top of the hill. There, I marveled at the magnificent panoramas and pondered the path we would take the next day. From this vantage point, I spotted the aging cypress[31] with its tall spire. I had set up camp under one of its branches on the southern bank of Lake Nahuel Huapi and its spire was supposed to lead my way back. However, what I saw seconds later

---

[30] It is currently thought that when the town of San Carlos de Bariloche was founded, the name "Bariloche" was mistakenly recorded rather than the allegedly correct Vuriloche. It is argued that the name Vuriloche derived from the pass discovered by Reverend P.J. Guillelmo in 1714 and rediscovered by Moreno in 1880. Curiously enough, the town of Bariloche was mapped out in 1902, and in 1883 Moreno published an article in La Nación newspaper in which he writes "Bariloche." "Bariloche" is used as well on maps published by the Argentine Geographic Institute, 1896 edition.

[31] The old cypress that still stands in San Carlos de Bariloche.

marred my vision of the near future. On the path cutting through the forest there stood a young Mapuche swinging his spear about freely. Upon setting eyes on me, he gave out a war cry I will never forget.

I was caught but was not unprepared. I had a plan I would follow if the grim predictions of both Indians and whites came to pass. In my role as leader of the expedition, I had to pull more than my weight because others depended on me. The exploratory commission had split up. On the one hand, it was imperative to take care of Bovio, the engineer, who was sick and had stayed in Tecka with half the men. It was a seven-day walk south to get to Inacayal and Foyel's huts, where he was recovering. Finally yet importantly were the five men who were waiting, sad-faced, by the cypress tree. Lacking ammunition, they would be unable to defend themselves. I finally reached them, escorted by the Indians who had somehow materialized from under the dense foliage where they had been secretly watching me. There were seventy-five of them led by Chuaiman, the son of Cacique Molfinqueupu ("Bloody Flint") and brother of the acting chief of the caravan taken captive by General Villegas. Inacayal's son Utrac, a loyal Indian who called himself "my brother," and Gavino, my interpreter and Shaihueque's distant relative, had stayed with my men to protect them from harm. The Indians claimed that they were there to ask a favor of me –with support from their spears, undoubtedly the best evidence we could possibly have as to the innocence of the prisoners held in Río Negro.[32] Their wish was to take me to Caleufú so that I could appeal to the national government for the release of those prisoners. In the meantime, I was to remain hostage. The spokesperson for the group was a crafty mixed-blood Valdivian and the most duplicitous man that has ever crossed the Andes: Loncochino, "Secretary of the

---

[32] These were the Indians who had slaughtered Lopez' troopers. Moreno had informed on them to General Conrado Villegas, who had immediately ordered their capture.

Supreme Government of Las Manzanas, Sir Valentín Shaihueque." I knew him well, however, and he indirectly played
a part in my plan. Above all, he wished to bring us before
Shaihueque in order to ingratiate himself with him and thus
regain the influence he had almost lost. He seemed delighted
to let me send three men (the bearers of my collections) with
an open letter to Bovio instructing him to join us in Caleufú.
He was unaware of the fact that I was also delivering a ver-
bal warning urging Bovio to stay put until further notice. In
that way, I was saving three men, while keeping the most
loyal by my side: José Melgarejo, Antonio Van Titter, Utrac,
and Gavino.

I knew that even if the government were to release the
prisoners, the Indians wouldn't let me go. I was too valuable
a hostage. Besides, I had reason to believe that not all prisoners would make it back to the Indian camp, so as we
marched, I devised a plan we would have to enforce without
fail. It required two-thirds of the expedition to escape when
they had the chance. Bovio would remain at his location. I
hoped to be able to advise him through Utrac, without Utrac
so realizing, as to the right time to slip away to Río Negro. It
seemed like a good strategy given the extremely long distance between my brave companion and the Mapuche huts.
I couldn't determine yet when the right time would be. I
would have to think about it after we arrived at Shaihueque's huts from Nahuel Huapi. Therefore, I urged Loncochino to speed up our march so I could write the letters as
soon as possible, but kept to myself the real reason for the
rush.

We would make our escape fifteen days after Bovio got the
message. What route would we take? I knew from the previous trip that there was an overland trail –one hundred miles
long– connecting Río Negro with Caleufú but it would be
impossible to travel the distance to the frontier. The path to
Chile was shorter but I was not unfamiliar with it at all. There
was no other alternative but to follow the course of the Limay
River. Villarino, the explorer, had gone up and down this

river in the previous century. I decided to take the river route myself. To our advantage, we wouldn't leave a trail in the water.

Two days later, we reached the Limay and stopped at the same spot where Musters had made his crossing, in close proximity to the site of Cox's shipwreck. Before us was the vessel that would carry us to safety: a raft made of branches used by the Indians for transporting their saddles while they swam, pulling and holding on to the sides. This raft would serve as a model for the one I was planning to launch in the Collón Curá. To swim with as much dexterity as the Indians was likely to arouse suspicion so I advised my helpers to tell the Indians that I felt ill and was a poor swimmer. When I stepped into the water, I acted as if my legs hurt badly and requested permission to climb on top of the raft rather than grab the submerged poles like everyone else. The Indians thought it was very funny but allowed me to do so, laughing at my weakness as illustrative of that of the whole white race.

Three hours later, we entered Caleufú valley. The huts were in the same place I had seen them in 1875-1876. From the top of the mountains, bonfires lit the sky signaling our arrival. We could hear the Indian warriors' constant yelling as they gathered at their meeting place. We stopped for a short while behind a hill next to the huts waiting for a sign that we could approach. I took advantage of the interval by hiding leftover food, two boxes of sardines and one of pâté, the barometer, and other instruments that might tip off the already wary Indians. Having done this, we approached and joined other groups coming from all over. They were armed and headed for the huts making disparaging remarks as they passed next to us. Their words didn't affect me as much as they hurt my friends Utrac and Gavino, who were walking silently beside me. These armed bands had failed to locate us and were envious of the more fortunate Chuaiman, who had led us here so their hatred towards us grew. Other Indians who had arrived before them were recovering their strength in front of the huts drinking warm blood from mares whose throats had just been cut open. The poor animals could not stop shaking and gushing blood all over the filthy wooden dishes placed under their necks.

After waiting for a while, during which time I was struck more than once by bones tossed into the bushes by one of the young prisoners' mother, wife or sister, Loncochino signaled that I could come into the hut by myself.

It was a critical moment. I would have to part with my two companions, drop my weapons, and walk through the hostile crowds that were already getting drunk on the Valdivian aguardiente with which they washed down the imbibed blood. I told my companions not to put up a fight if stripped of the Remington rifles or my luggage. Neither should they act at all frightened if they heard screaming coming from the hut. I instructed them to refuse to let the Indians touch their clothes, though. Indians have a lot of respect for the value of the individual. I was counting on being able to invoke that belief and avoid humiliation.

I raised the skin that covered the entrance to the big hut. Shaihueque was lying against some cushions on the fur mattress that served both as his throne and as his bed. It faced the "stalls" of his five women. Not knowing what to make of my visit, the Cacique got up and reached out to me with his hand but I refused to shake it.

"My friend, aren't you going to shake your right hand with me?" he asked.

"No, my friend," I said, determined to take a stand in this encounter by proving that this "white fox" was too smart to fall for Indian finagling.

His fierce smile froze; his face bore the expression of an arrogant lion. Visibly upset, he called out to Loncochino in a strained voice.

Loncochino showed up within seconds. He must have been eavesdropping. All the chiefs and chieftains whose responsibility had been to look for me, a job they had performed with varying degrees of success, followed his lead.

Among them were the brave "Condor of the East," (Puelmanque), Molfinqueupu, and the ferocious Chacayal, my former nemesis. They came in and took their respective places, commensurate with the stature they held at the Council. Little by little, the hut filled up with about a hundred warriors gathered to listen to the prisoner's "reasons."

Looking back on that day, I cannot say that I felt completely at ease. For one, those half-naked men, their faces and chests smeared in paint, their long hair bristling with falcon feathers, were moving about nervously as if sniffing blood. Then most were related to the prisoners of Río Negro. Their slings and bolas hanging from their belts, they dug holes in the ground with their long facones or large knives.

Dressed as I was in a sergeant major's uniform, I reminded them of battles where they had lost more than a few "peñi" (brothers). For me it was an honor to wear the national flag around my chest under my shirt. However, the revolver hanging down from my neck and hidden behind my back[33] posed a major problem. If anyone saw it, we would be in serious trouble. Nevertheless, we weren't thinking about it under the circumstances.

We had lined up in a row. Loncochino, Flandés, the Valdivian silversmith, and the Chilean Indian Cochi-Miguel, who knew Spanish and could grasp my words, had positioned themselves in front. Utrac and Gavino sat silently at each side of me, like repentant sinners –as far as the Mapuches were concerned, sinned they had, merely by accompanying the

---

[33] Some of these clothes are kept in the "Founder's Room" at the La Plata Museum. I still have in my possession the revolver with its scarcely legible engraving -made with a needle- bearing the following signatures and reference points: Las Flores, Azul, Roldán, Indio Rico, Bahía Blanca, Punta Alta, Nueva Roma, Salinas; Río Colorado, Patagones, Bahía San Blas, Aguada de los Loros, Guardia General Mitre, Bajada de Balcheta, and Choele Choel Island, Chichinal, Cheynal Geyú, Río Limay, Chaleún Geyú, Choica Geyú, Fuen Geyú, Ranquil, Trimnao, Collón Curá, Caleufú, Nahuel Huapi, F.P. Moreno 1875, Chilchiuma, Quem Quim Luen, Chimehuin, October 4, '80, Pilcan, Pungei Lien, Quelen Geyú, Buenos Aires. E.V.M.

enemy here. Shaihueque repeated: "My friend," but I did not respond so he stood up –the same frozen smile on his face– and spoke to his Indians in Araucan.

"Loncochino, what does the Cacique say to this?

"My Superior Government says: Look at the hueza-huinca (ugly, wretched Christian man). He is scared speechless. His teeth are chattering."

The Indians grinned. After Loncochino translated these words, it was my turn.

"Since when did you start treating Christians like dogs? Before making a Christian talk, you're supposed to feed him." This is a Mapuche formality and I was sticking to it in this situation especially because food was scarce.

The elders started to mumble something and then stopped. My good friend Fia, old Musters's savior, brought me the customary but no less disgusting dish of raw mare liver sprinkled with salt and chili pepper. Once I had eaten everything on my plate, the long "parliament" began, with Gavino and Loncochino acting as interpreters. I told Loncochino:

"Tell my friend he can start talking."

"Why didn't the Christian send messengers advising he was in Mapuche territory? Why is he hiding his people and keeping his distance from us? Could it be that he is mean-spirited and out to harm the owners of this land? Why is he engaging in witchcraft in the big lake? (When I arrived in Nahuel Huapi I found a small dog in the forest, a mongrel, who, lured by the smell of meat, joined us at the campsite. The first group of Indians that approached found no better or more natural explanation for its presence than to surmise that I had made it rise from the lake.)

"Answer why! If you don't, you're a dog!"

"Loncochino, tell Shaihueque that the only dogs here are the Indians. They are dogs that wag their tails before they bark. Why do you send for me as a friend and then treat me like an enemy? Nobody came to meet us when we arrived. What's more, your people have been hurling insults at us. Had I suspected this would happen I wouldn't have come!"

Chacayal gave out an angry roar when he heard I was calling him a dog. "I would have crawled like a snake to get to the ugly Christian. Chacayal is not afraid of the F'ta Tralcan" (big thunder). He was referring to the theodolite. For some it resembled cannon that could kill one hundred men at a time. For others it was a suspicious device that worked in connection with the sun to make my witchcraft possible.

After this first outburst cleared the air, I stated my position in no uncertain terms.

"Loncochino, tell my friend Shaihueque that he is not going to get what he wants from me. He demands that I appeal to the government for the release of his Indians. But can I say with any certainty that they are innocent? Do I run the government? Would the government believe someone who writes without the benefit of his freedom? I would have to tell the truth that the Mapuches are no longer friendly to the government. Would you expect me to stay until all the prisoners returned? That would be forever because I have no intention of writing. My friend Shaihueque tells me that I am worth a lot in my country. Who has told him that? The government could not care less if I ever returned! I could be replaced by anybody from the thousands of men there. There's only a few of you here but the imprisoned Indians are many. Go ahead and be enemies of all the Christians; they will soon do away with you! Indian bones outnumber ours in the sun-bleached heaps that dot the countryside. If I ever get out of here, I will see you all imprisoned in Buenos Aires. Pincen is waiting for you!

Does my friend Shaihueque remember the "tapayu" horse and the spear that he once gave me when we were friends? There's a portrait depicting Toro Pincen, as they call him here. That portrait of him with the spear serves as a mask or "collón" to scare the young.

Does my friend remember Cisnal's shirt, made of seven skins, the one Chocorí, his father, tossed out when he ran away from a bunch of Christians in Río Negro, while carrying him in his arms? Does he remember it? Well, I have it at home. It is white with red stripes. Am I correct? What, on the other hand, do the Mapuches have that they have taken from us Christians? They only have what I have given them as friendship gifts. Have Shaihueque send Chacayal to look for my men's rifles. My carbine is under my saddle padding. Take it as my gift to him. Take everything and then see whether your friend has fear in his heart or his teeth chatter!

I was putting my life on the line by adopting this attitude but the situation prompted me to do so. Shaihueque fell silent. Chacayal did not. He came forward and stood between the two campfires burning in the middle of the hut. From there he addressed the silent captains: "The Christian here is very mean when he talks to us like this. If instead of being alone he were with his people he wouldn't even notice us."

The test was not over yet. I was glad I had disregarded Loncochino and Flandes' advice. They had told me that too much haughtiness might lead to something bad. However, my words had helped me avoid a humiliating situation. I could not wish for anything more.

The dialogue continued in like tone for several hours as the lords of the plains and their prisoners hashed over the same subject. The Indians exaggerated their strengths while I focused on ours.

"F'vinte (Vintter) is very strong. A real bull!"

"F'Viyega (Villegas) is very strong. A real bull!"

"Or-tega. He's a real bull too!"

In the end, I gave in and, as proof that I harbored no ill feelings towards the Indians, I promised to write the next day. The Indians spared my life and Shaihueque gained control of the situation.

My plan was moving along fine until I ran into the first difficulty. Where would I sleep? It would have been crazy to try to escape from inside the hut. Our only chance depended on us getting back the tent I had given to them as a gift in the past. I had to make them believe my condition had worsened.

Utrac and Gavino helped me obtain the tent even though Shaihueque said I should live like an Indian, just as I had done in previous occasions.

When I was out again I saw my two helpers, their heads high though unarmed and surrounded by a curious crowd.

"Señor, they took our weapons but they are afraid of the theodolite. They tried to take our jackets too but they would have had to do so over our dead bodies. We almost rushed in when we heard shouting. We thought you were being murdered."

"I would have 'taken care' of Shaihueque first," said the brave Melgarejo from Entre Ríos.

"Good thinking!" added Antonio, the Belgian veteran from Paraguay.

These two loyal men were aware of my plan and had faith in it. They were anxious to help Utrac and Gavino pitch the tent. They finished so quickly that it was already set up in front of Shaihueque's hut when he came out. Four meters apart and facing east, no other huts blocking the view. In Melgarejo's words, whispered into my ear, "the coast was clear for the final sprint."

It was in our best interest for the five of us to sleep inside the tent that first night, regardless of how small it was. Cochi-Miguel and an Indian who was loyal to Utrac lay across the entrance. No guards were watching us since an escape on foot made no sense at all, given the distance between the frontier and us.

Of course, Utrac was in the dark concerning my escape plan, since he would have never allowed it. He was sure the Indians would return and that he would be able to accompany me back. I took advantage of his unsuspecting kindness and made plans to save Bovio. When the noise died down and everybody fell asleep, I persuaded him that Bovio should be advised to leave for Choele-Choel immediately. Once there, he should try to influence General Villegas. Under no circumstances must Shaihueque learn of this plot, which would ultimately benefit the prisoners if "my brother Utrac" dared to send an Indian carrying a concealed letter. As soon as he and I reached an understanding, I wrote a brief note in French to my good friend Bovio warning him that he had fifteen days to pack up and go. I said I would attempt to escape as soon as possible as well. It was midnight and using a page from my journal, I wrote under a blanket in complete darkness. At the break of day, I noticed the errors I had made so I rewrote it and kept the first draft as a memento of those unhappy times.

At noon, Utrac marched off at a slow pace so as not to arouse suspicion. He carried the small piece of paper hidden in the rag he was using as "huincha" (headband) to tie up his hair.

It was January 27 and we had until February 10. There was no rush. I slept and continued to feel under the weather the rest of the day. The following day, Loncochino impatiently demanded that I write to the government.

"How am I supposed to write without paper or ink? I said. When you provide those, I will, not just to the president but also to influential friends.

I spent the 28th and 29th writing. Shaihueque and Loncochino kept interrupting me. They expected me to write volumes to prove that the captives were innocent. The secretary stood guard making sure I did not keep any pieces of paper for myself.

The messengers were leaving on the 30th. They were ready at noon and so was I. I had written two identical letters to Vintter that night, both of which were in French. One was for Antonio to carry inside his tattered jacket collar. The other I placed under Melgarejo's shabby saddle. If at least one of them arrived at its intended destination, it would be almost a total victory. I instructed Vintter to dismiss the letters requesting the release of the prisoners. Instead, he was to detain the messenger and leave us to our own devices. I trusted my own strength and did not want to take part in an exchange. It would have been quite disgraceful. I wonder if General Vintter has kept my letter. I only had to cross out two words from it after Loncochino read it aloud inside the hut, an exercise in futility, as nobody there understood Spanish. In the letter to Lucio López, I wrote that I had named one of our "national treasures ," the snow-covered peak that dominated the campsite by the lake, after his grandfather. The words "gloria patria" rang suspicious to the poor fellow, an ex parish sexton raised in a Chilean mission. "Gloria patri," he repeated to himself. "There's something wrong here," he stated. Therefore, I had to erase it and change it. I do not know if Lucio has kept the note.

As I said, everything was set to go and the messengers were about to leave. The question was how to send Antonio on his way as well.

"Tell me, my friend, will your people be able to obtain safe passage to the fort area?"

Upon hearing my question, Loncochino panicked. He quickly admitted with embarrassment that he had not thought about it.

"I'll provide safe passage," I said, "because I do want things to go well for my friend here." On a sheet of paper I wrote a letter to the fort commander (I did not have a clue whether there was one or not) ordering him to take good care of the messengers. Still, Shaihueque needed more reassurance.

"Do you think somebody will hurt them?

"I don't know, my friend. If they manage to escape detection, they might be spared. However, if soldiers see them they will fire. You are the enemy now."

Both the Cacique and secretary were stunned. My harsh logic was hard to swallow, but I saved the day by suggesting the following: "Why not send one of my men? I think Antonio knows the fort area. Although I'm sick and could use his services, I'm willing to let him go in the interest of this mission." Moments later Antonio was getting ready to mount. He looked confused but I had forewarned him so he held on to the back of his jacket collar where he had concealed the secret note. The Indians had made a list for him as well. He was to bring back sugar, mate, sheet metal, ponchos, fine boots, etc, mostly for the secretary. My good Belgian friend took off without exchanging a single word with me. Shortly afterwards I could see they had crossed the Caleufú and were going up the trail that leads to the Limay. It was a beautiful afternoon and I spent a long time gazing at the distance, my eyes on Antonio. It was now his turn to march towards safety.

Melgarejo, Gavino, and I were left behind for the time being. So far, there had been no visible reaction among the Indiàns, but the following day brought some changes. Messengers were running around the green valley in a cloud of dust. One piece of bad news followed another. That night we got word that Colonel Ortega's division was preparing to invade.

No matter how friendly they may seem, there is always a spy or two lurking among the Indians. In the morning messengers announced that a letter written in Spanish had been found in the Lonquimay area. The missive, which had come unexpectedly, said that God protected the Indians. Proof of this could be found in Chile, where a whole city had burnt down, according to the letter. Then another messenger warned that the Indians would die as had been forecast that very afternoon by the February 1880 comet that could be seen shining brightly through an Andean gorge.

In response to these events, Shaihueque decided to call the Council of War of Quem-Quem-Treu. The subject of the meeting would be how to best prepare for Antonio's return. On our way there the next day, we ran into an Indian who had escaped from Río Negro. He told us how two others had been shot to death as they attempted to escape with him. I had to admit our situation was getting worse by the minute.

In the early morning of the third, we came down to the plain. The golden rays of the sun were warming up the snow-capped peak of the gigantic Quetropillán. All the warriors summoned to the meeting were in attendance. It would take too long to describe the "Aucatrahum;" I will have to do so some other time. I will just say for now that after a series of military maneuvers and a head count that rendered 800 Indians where I had only seen 480, the ritual ended. A mock attack on the frontier ensued. The Indians speared grassy shrubs prying them out of the soil as if they were toppling their poor Christian victims one by one at Fta Loncó's (great mind) command, that is to say on Shaihueque's orders. Then the big circle of captains came together.

I will always remember that scene. I tried to fend off the older warriors' accusations, further aggravated by the prompt arrival of two of Namuncurá's messengers, who had come to ask for help against Colonel Ortega (I've seen one of them at the barracks lately.) Somebody shot a stone with a shingshot and it whizzed by me, barely missing my big ears. Spearheads tickled my chest. It was an unbearable situation, but I knew that if I panicked and moved, however slightly, I would be lost. Everything seemed stacked against me, even my old friend Ñancucheuque. That fearless cacique, who caused the most harm to the army two years later, had missed the meeting because he was on bad terms with Shaihueque. He had asked Shaihueque for an exorbitant price to redress the death of Ñancucheuque's son-in-law killed during a drinking spree by an Indian from Shaihueque's tribe. He demanded thirteen horses, thirteen silver garments, and two slaves, one of whom should not only be female, but should also have to be the slayer's daughter. Ñancucheuque also wanted to know why I was still alive.

The meeting ended with a resolution. Indian forces would occupy all roads near the border and get ready for combat. There is always something ludicrous happening at these ceremonies as well. On this occasion, the resolution called for all unmarried daughters to be given "in matrimony" to whoever requested their hand, whether rich or poor, since there was a need to increase the number of strong able-bodied men. If this wise measure ended up succeeding, it probably resulted in a few extra young people among those who have recently surrendered.

I was hopeful I would be able to escape by sailing down the river but I needed to see it again so I could orient myself. It had been four years since I had last been there. I managed to get the group to return to the huts by way of the river. My inquisitiveness had paid off. From our location in the foothills of the Andes, I had repeatedly asked whether a stream I could see between the mountains was the Valdivia pass. Later as I stepped onto the trail I had been so eager to reach, I forgot all about the "Parliament." The Indians were laughing at me as I crossed over streams feigning ineptness, falling into holes, and getting soaked. Nevertheless, my eyes were fixed on the voluminous waters of the Collón Curá. I did not miss a single twist or turn. When I arrived at the tent where Melgarejo was waiting, he looked aghast at the muddy condition of my clothes and could tell I had been scouting around for a suitable "point of departure." I confided the good news to my loyal helper. That afternoon we only ate "noodles" made of an old leather halter, but it did not matter to us. It was a relief to know we would soon be free. We had made the decision to flee and would soon execute it.

THE GETAWAY

While we conferred at Quem-Quem-Treu, one of the three distinguished medicine men summoned by Shaihueque arrived in Caleufú from Chile. He was to preside over the rogations to the great F'ta Huentrú (The Great Man) and the revered Antú (the sun). These prayers were much needed because there was a widespread expectation that tumultuous times were ahead. The other two medicine men had refused to attend. They were afraid to face a "male witch" as strong as I was. Even the most daring one avoided me when I returned to the tent. He preferred to go to a dense thicket by the side of the river to carry out his evocations. He waited there until the night of the fourth. Once the pouch made of a cow's stomach was filled with magic stones, the "rali" or drum and the drumsticks were in place, and everything was ready, his raucous performance began.

Based on the horrible moaning and groaning that filled the stillness of the night, it was obvious that the male witch was not having much luck winning over the beautiful soothsayer of 1876, as his "walichus" did not rush over with the long-expected news. It was not until dawn, and after he had succumbed to exhaustion that he spoke:

"The Christians are invading!"

When Shaihueque heard the news, he sent Loncochino to wake me up. In my dreams, I could hear friendly clarinets playing reveille at the top of the mountain but instead, I had to persuade the half-asleep, half-dressed Indians around me that the wizard's predictions were wrong. He could not possibly know more than I did, now could he! He had shown he valued my opinion when he said I was a powerful wizard who had moved the huge sacred stone, symbol of Shaihueque's power and strong leadership. If the rock had rolled off –and it almost did– Shaihueque's power would have been crushed and it would all have been my doing, according to the "machi."

I urged Shaihueque to give the "machi" the means to fine tune his predictions. Immediately, a new drum and drumstick were conjured up. After a series of frenzied drumbeats and ear-piercing yells, my enraptured colleague jumped from a tree that served as his temple. A surge of excitement raced through him as he modified his previous forecast. Although it was true that the army was on the prowl, it was Namuncurá's settlement that was being targeted.

The good news brought about a sense of relief that was short-lived. At noon, we learned that a messenger had drowned in the Collón-Curá. It was presumed that the Christians had chased him down to the river. When the first fugitive families arrived, they brought alarming though contradictory news and my situation deteriorated.

The prayer sessions started on the sixth. I have described this ritual in my "Viaje a la Patagonia Austral," (Journey to Southern Patagonia) to which the inquisitive reader can refer. The only difference is that the spirit of war was more prevalent during the current ceremony. For example, as they sprayed their spears with liquor the old captains prayed for strength in their right hand to pierce the "huincas' " chests.

We chose the same site used in 1876, between the huts and the Collón-Curá. The trail was dotted with firewood and it became our escape route. Where there is wood, there are branches with which to build rafts.

Gavino had already removed the precious cargo we had disposed of upon our arrival at the huts, and which we now had to place somewhere along our escape path. Pretending I was in worse health still than before, I complained that I was cold –even though I was wrapped up in a poncho– and pretended I could barely walk, so much so that I had to be held up by Gavino and Melgarejo. Despite their help in getting through the crowd headed for "Camaricun," I had to stop and rest under a pepper tree. By the time I got up, the three cans were safely under the sand. Nobody became suspicious.

It would serve no purpose to talk about the coarse language heard that day during the feast. On the second day, I arrived on horseback. Shaihueque was convinced that I could not walk. On the third day, he would not let me out of my tent. Something very serious was in the air, as I learnt that night from Gavino.

The "machi" had contacted his most powerful "walichus". After several trips to and from Choele-Choel for conversations with the spirits of General Villegas and Colonel Vintter, they related that many of the captives were dead. The remaining ones would not be returning to the huts because I had surreptitiously written a letter demanding they be denied their freedom. I had in fact done so and it was easy to figure it out. The seer was Loncochino's compatriot (a Christian who had once asked for "holy water" to rid a suffering man from the evil spirits in his stomach.) He reckoned that Antonio must have been the bearer of a covert warning. A while later, the Indians' death was confirmed by a second escapee.

Lengthy discussions followed regarding what should be done with us. The wicked medicine man argued that I had to be killed to atone for the Indians' deaths. I was to be savagely tormented, my heart gouged out at the water's edge. But Shaihueque was opposed. He wanted no part of it, because his father, Chocorí, on his deathbed, explained that he had been "wrapped in Christian garments" as a baby and ordered him never to stain his hands with the blood of a Christian. In addition, I was his *compadre*, so why not wait for the messenger's return (the one that never would, according to the seer.) Meanwhile, the sacrificial offering would require double the number of slaughtered animals.

That night while we rested, glad to have increased our provisions with some sheep's lard for which I had traded my only extra shirt, I was awakened by a noise near the tent. Two knife-wielding Indians were crawling towards us. Perhaps they were relatives of the ones that died. The moment we got up, though, they were gone.

We knew that we had to flee or face death before it was too late. Shaihueque told me during one of our quasi-friendly talks that since our government had cut off the rations he no longer wielded the same influence over his people. In addition, even though he would never hurt me, the time might come when he would be unable to defend me from some of his chieftains. Perhaps he was thinking of Chacayal. This terrible situation declined even further the next day. As soon as the day broke, I sent Gavino to ask Shaihueque for a horse to take me to the "Villatun" sacrificial ceremony. I wanted to feign ignorance about what was going on and act nonchalantly.

I waited in vain until I saw dust clouds in the distance, which signaled the approaching troupe with its strange cast of characters, (Buenos Aires was celebrating Carnival that Monday.) The bloody orgy was over. The drunken and vociferous crowd was coming back home in a sea of voices rising to thunderous cries and then falling. Melgarejo and I could hear the loud, insulting words "Hueza huinca."

I had left my revolver with the canned food and had no other weapons.

"Boss, are we going to be killed?" Melgarejo asked.

"I bet they would kill us if they could."

Having said that I emerged from my tent at the exact moment in which Shaihueque and Chacayal, already intoxicated, were coming at us. One yell from me was enough to stop them.

"Why didn't you bring me a horse?" I asked.

He patted his as he mumbled.

"Been losing... horses... my friend."

A satisfactory answer that ruled out, perhaps, any criminal intent. Shaihueque tried to dismount but stirrups can be tricky after several shots of *aguardiente*. He fell down and rolled all the way to the entrance of my tent. I doubted anyone would dare step over him.

Chacayal still bellowed but nobody listened. The women laid down their blankets around the tent and the drinking began. We remained at the center. I remember that day and that night in all the gory details. We were alone, Melgarejo and I. Utrac and Gavino were getting drunk in the other huts. Every now and then, we heard voices through the cracks –we had closed off the entrance with thorns. "Here they come to kill you!" Outside it was mayhem even though the women had picked up the weapons. We managed to escape. My poncho was the only casualty. It was stabbed and torn to shreds.

On the morning of the 10th, the events of the night still hung in the air. Drunks were lying around everywhere. There were women weeping. The wounded were crying vengeance at the top of their voices. The situation could not last. It was time for the warriors to go back to the valleys in order to defend them. Enough was enough. By the afternoon, Caleufú was deserted. The savages were exhausted and, under the circumstances, the plan we had so patiently drawn up would soon have to be put in motion. The time had come.

The question was how to escape without being noticed by Utrac, Cochi-Miguel, and Rauque, the guard, who was already watching us.

Doctor Pirovano had assembled a collection of small bottles filled with heavy doses of chloral and potassium bromide. I had one of them on me. Utrac is a fine Indian but he is too fond of liquor. On more than one occasion, he has asked me for permission to get drunk. He was crestfallen that afternoon because there was no more alcohol left. I jumped at the chance of being the purveyor of the precious liquid.

"Hey, brother, why don't you drink "michipulcú?" (an intoxicating beverage made of some sort of fermented pepper.)

"It ain't strong enough. No high."

"You must have tried it cold. Have you ever had it hot?"

"No, brother."

"Well, I'll prepare it for you. You'll see what I mean. It's a lot stronger but it tastes great."

We immediately put the boiler on. I emptied the bottle and put in equal amounts of seeds and water, which made for a potent drink capable of burning the throat of the most hardened seaman. One couldn't even taste the chloral because this concoction was pepper extract, somewhat worse than terebinth tree infusion. I tried it myself so as not to arouse suspicion. The three Indians consumed the rest. Night had fallen and we tried to rest. Soon we would feel drowsy.

There was not a soul walking outside. The weather was unsettled; it was a dark cloudy night. The dogs were sleeping indoors. We could only hear the wizard's monotonous chanting and the old women's sustained wailing coming from inside Shaihueque's "house." He was healing Cachul, who had fallen sick after the orgy.

Inside the tent, Melgarejo, Gavino, and I pretended to be asleep. Utrac, Cochi-Miguel, and Rauque had a bad case of chloral-induced snoring. Our plan was as follows: I would leave first and head towards the pepper trees along the loose stone path (Ya-laley-curá-stones that make noise) in the dry riverbed. That way I would leave no footsteps. Afterwards I would pick up the revolver and boxes. Gavino would soon follow and shortly thereafter, it would be Melgarejo's turn. He would first have to steal a lasso from a horse grazing nearby. Once we were all together, we would go to the river to look for sticks and make a raft.

I left according to plan. My nerves had sharpened my sense of hearing. I was able to perceive the slightest stir. I still remember the increasingly loud noise of the loose stones knocking against each other as they rolled down the dry gulch. When I got to the pepper tree, I unearthed the revolver and cleaned it right away. I put the three boxes in my pocket and then thought back on my last few steps. What would happen if my companions were caught?

It was Tuesday and Buenos Aires was celebrating Carnival that week. I unwittingly turned my attention to all those things I had affection for there. I stroked the place in my chest where I kept the flag, my journals, and the pictures of my loving friends.[34]

---

[34] Among them, his sister Maruja's portrait, which, along with other docu-

Time passed and I did not hear the slightest noise, except for a dog barking in the distance. What an ordeal!

The river dropped down a few meters ahead. There was a fork made by two tree branches that would come in handy if I needed protection during an attack. I checked my bullets one by one. Eighteen cartridges easily fit into the six barrels. If I had sufficient time to fire them all, the cost of an attempt on my life would be quite high. One hour passed, then two, and then three. Hidden in my hair under the knot in the dirty and torn scarf I had tied around my head, my watch marked time as I waited for Gavino and Melgarejo, but they never came.

Shortly after midnight, the noise of the rolling stones got increasingly louder. I heard a horse coming. It was my good helper on a pony.

"Chief, Gavino refuses to leave. He's afraid. Says the seer found out about your letter and will now be able to predict which road we've taken."

It was typical Indian logic.

What should we do? We couldn't go it alone. Gavino would betray me. Therefore, I decided to return to the tent. I buried the boxes again but kept the revolver. We would have to try again the following day anyway.

I will let the reader decide whether I got discouraged. Utrac was still asleep. Gavino was silent. The wizard kept up his chanting.

My boots were wet from crossing the stream in front of the tent so I could not get up that morning. The Indians would have become suspicious. Shaihueque came to visit while I lay on the animal skin that served as my bed. He rarely visited me inside my tent. He had too much respect for the theodolite case and the mysterious box I used for a pillow. Still, he wanted to know if I had suffered during the drinking binge. By that time, the events of the previous night were a blur and

---

ments, escaped intact from the fire that burned while they rested on the island during their escape by raft along the Rio Limay.

he was unusually polite. I had run out of chloral and would have to find a way to keep Utrac at bay while I persuaded Gavino to escape that night.

"My friend, don't you think it would be a good idea for Utrac to return to Inacayal's huts?" I asked Shaihueque. I expect the imprisoned Indians will soon be back and since I am quite sure that the Mapuches will keep their word, I will go back to Río Negro. However, for this, I need to have all my people and for Utrac to bring fifty young men from his father's camp so they can defend us from Namuncurá on our journey.

It was a clever idea and Shaihueque saw that it would be in his best interest to separate Utrac from Gavino. Ultrac agreed to the proposal and we made plans to meet fifteen days later.

When Shaihueque left, it didn't take long before I was able to convince Gavino that the seer's predictions were pure nonsense. "After all," I said, "did he ever notice we tried to escape last night, or that we will be leaving the tent again tonight?" I did not think so!

He could not argue with my reasoning. The good Indian apologized and swore obedience in all future endeavors. I ordered him to go to Shaihueque's hut to tell him he wanted to leave too, and that he would catch up with Utrac the next day, since he did not want to leave me behind when I was so sick. He was to repeat this at all the surrounding huts where he would go to say good-bye. Then he would complain that he didn't have enough horses and try to get two from Utrac before coming back to see me. My boots were still wet and I should not be seen in them. I sent someone to ask Loncochino for some reading material. The only book he owned was a dirty copy of "The Life of Saint Genevieve." I read it to pass the time. How could anyone distrust me or think there was a conspiracy under way while I was engrossed in this story?

Hunger pangs hindered our progress while we planned our escape and forced us to search the grass for grease droplets left over from past barbecues. One man's garbage is another man's treasure. This dog food kept our hands off the precious cargo of lard that we were setting aside in case we had to go without for a long time before we reached the frontier. We had to feed our hunger somehow so we were thrilled to see that a mare was being slaughtered and wasted no time helping ourselves to the entrails our good friend Fia sneaked out for us. We devoured them even though they were barely roasted. We felt more confident on a full stomach.

As soon as the "machi" loaded the meat, he mounted and rode off. Gavino looked on until he lost sight of him. Then he turned to me and said:

"He didn't have a clue, Chief!"

Utrac was leaving then, so I asked Gavino to accompany him for a while and then come back through the wooded area. He was to take the horses to the good grassland above the banks of the Collón-Curá, next to the spot used by Shaihueque to trap ostriches with his boleadoras across from the Moncol range. There he would find timber to make the raft to transport our saddles. He would return at sundown after having let one horse go and he would tie up his mount to a pole by the tent. I must confess that my main concern was leaving no trace. If I managed to put the savages off for two days, the success of my mission would be practically assured.

We planned to slip away that very night. We would lead them to think we had taken off with Utrac, who was a fast walker. The two horses' hoof prints would point them in the wrong direction.

After Utrac and Gavino left I went with Shaihueque to the choeca (Indian hockey) playing field. Melgarejo remained. He was asleep inside the tent, a stolen lasso concealed underneath his body. His and Gavino's would serve to secure the logs in the soon-to-be-built raft. Rauque, the guard, had a bad cough, and I persuaded him to do something about it. Luckily for us he went to bed. We did not want to have to watch our backs the whole time. He was a well-known assassin, later shot to death right at that spot by Colonel Ortega's forces.

I stood by Shaihueque for three hours as he lay on the

ground happily watching his able-bodied men practice their skills. My legs hurt so much I could not sit down. I was in shirtsleeves and the large Smith and Wesson revolver hung down my back under the shirt. If I so much as leaned the wrong way, the barrel would give me away.

When the sun went down behind the silver backdrop of the T'chilchiuma, and the Cordillera cast its cold shadows over us I became discouraged. Would I ever get to see the light of day again?

I met with Gavino back at the tent. He had "everything ready" and the horse was tied up. We felt like convicts getting their last meal before being executed. We had not been convicted but we felt close to death so I asked my friend Shai-hueque for a piece of meat. He brought it, roasted it for me, and availed himself of a few bites of our last supper. For a while we joked around about the ball game scheduled for the next day in the area and I laughed to myself at the prospect of getting soaked when I made the raft crossing. Then Fia called out to him to come to dinner and we said good-bye. "Have a good night, my friend," I said. "See you tomorrow…" (Or five years later!)

There were three of us left in the tent to coordinate the getaway. Gavino would leave first this time. If caught he would say he was going to a nearby hut. If he made it he would wait for us by the pepper tree. After a precautionary interval in which I would count from "one to one hundred," Melgarejo and I would follow. If an Indian overheard us and approached our tent, Melgarejo would say that Gavino was out and that I was sleeping. The theodolite was covered with blankets to make it look like my body was lying there.

We got ready to leave. I fixed up the brown and white blanket[35] –a gift from Inacayal that had been pierced by the drunken Indian's knife during the drinking spree. I took out the lard from under the leather skin and grabbed the

---

[35] It is housed at the La Plata Museum.

revolver. Melgarejo ran his finger over the edge of the knife and found the lasso. I ordered Gavino to come out slowly and saddle the horses right away. It was a cold, starry night, yet dark. The bonfires burning inside the huts blocked the outside view. The dogs were lying around the fires, their eyes set on their hidden bones, their busy tongues licking the pots and dishes. There was not a soul in range. The coast was clear.

Gavino emerged carrying a saddle on his shoulder but stepped back inside moments later.

"The horse is frightened," he said. "Won't budge and won't let me go near him."

We would have to take our chances. We had to make the horse move, so I went out to spook him. I was ready to start running after him if necessary. I dragged my poncho behind me like an Indian girl.[36] Nobody heard us leave, but when the horse jumped over the stream it splashed water and the dogs barked. Gavino dropped the halter and ran to a hiding place behind the rocks. It was a critical moment. If caught I was doomed. I instinctively threw myself down and grabbed hold of the horse. The meek, hungry horse began to nibble at the grass. The dogs kept barking so I could not move. Five minutes passed. An Indian leaned out the door of the big hut, looked around but went back inside, his eyes unable to adjust to the blinding darkness. What was he thinking? Had he concluded the horse was loose and was gloating on Gavino waking up to find he would have to walk all the way? The dogs were silent now. They had gone back to rest beside the fire so I began to drag myself forward slowly, while making the horse walk as if it were still loose. A shaken Gavino was waiting for me. When I reached him we saddled and mounted the horse, then headed for the pepper tree.

"Here I am, Chief. I am so sorry I had to leave the theodo-

---

[36] Magnificent garment Moreno had restored after he returned from his travels.

lite behind. We were almost caught!" It was Melgarejo speaking.

The die had been cast. I dug the three boxes out of the sand and told the loyal Melgarejo to get behind Gavino while I held on to the horse's tail. For weight I had tied three stones to the edge of the poncho so it would sweep over our tracks. Then we took off through the firewood that rimmed the path. As far as the Indians were concerned we had vanished. They might even have agreed with the seer that he who disappeared without a trace must no doubt be a wizard. We kept going like this for a few minutes across the celebration grounds until we reached the dunes by the river where there was no way we could erase our steps. We could hear loud shouting coming from the Indian camp a few hundred meters away. The Indians used burning logs as large torches. We could see their reflection but there was no sound of approaching footsteps. They had discovered we were missing but had no idea where we had gone.

I found an errant rock before entering the quicksand area and climbed on top of it, wiping off my footprints with my poncho. Then I told Gavino to go to the log site with Melgarejo. Once the raft was built, he was to come back for me. We would leave no sign of our presence except for a horse that would wander south in search of Utrac, his master.

I was alone on the rock. The shrieking continued; the stars seemed to shine more brightly; the mountains, black sinister shapes, were visible in the sky. I wondered what our fate would be when we reached the rushing waters of the Limay. We had escaped from the Indians. Would death be waiting in the river? In my thoughts I could see Buenos Aires as a distant point in the horizon.

Gavino returned at ten thirty. He was happy. The raft was almost ready and it had nine willow branches that would deliver us to safety. Ten minutes later we let the horse go and joined Melgarejo. After concluding our preparations, we floated our wooden remnant of the infancy of navigation on the Collón Curá. Before we jumped on board, I stopped to pick up a souvenir from this remote spot. It would prove that we were not afraid that night. I wanted a flower, and I went to cut it from among the rocks on the riverbank. I still have it before me as I write. Its colors have faded but it still vividly reminds me of the theatre of the wilderness.

When we climbed onto the raft it sank three quarters of the way but it did not occur to us that we would not make it. We were laughing to our hearts' content as we sailed downstream at a dizzying speed.

"Good-bye Caleufú," we chanted. Our words were drowned by the noise of the waves as they crashed over the first rocks lying on the river bottom just below the surface, pulling us down until I lost my shoes. The Collón Curá carries most of the snowmelt from the Andes. In this fast-flowing river, the raft would smoothly glide over the deep-running waters and then list as it rode the waves around the rocky bends. We had been "sailing" like this for a mere two hours when we heard screaming coming from the huts along the western bank. At the same time an avalanche of water hit us. This powerful force pushed us to the foot of the huge mountain where the churning waves whirled around protruding rocks. The raft foundered and ran aground between two of the rocks. There was a loud rattling noise, and since it was pitch black we could only see the white foam. We had to get out of this infernal river, dead or alive, before daylight, or else the Indians would find us. All three of us understood that, but each in his own way. My two companions shed their clothes; Gavino dropped his revolver and Melgarejo responded by letting go of the knife. They wanted to climb over the rocks and flee on foot, but I objected. Compared to them I was carrying a lot of weight: the wide belt with 40 cartridges, the revolver, the flag, the travel journals, the lard, and the 3 boxes. Before letting go of the logs, I searched underneath for the obstruction that had brought us to a halt. As I pushed against the flow, the strong current propelled the raft forward and caused it to slide off the rocks. As a result, the raft righted itself and was violently carried away by the rushing waters. I scraped my legs on the rocks and suffered from these injuries for months. However, I was glad to be sailing down the wide river again.

Approximately at two in the morning we spotted the Río Limay. It flows from the south and is fed by the Collón Curá before heading towards the northeast. As we entered the part of the river closest to the border, the light of Venus shone on the water that receded into the horizon. I was paralyzed with terrible back pain caused by having exerted myself, so Melgarejo had to prop me up or else I would have fallen in. Fortunately, before dawn, we were able to maneuver down the river to an island dominated by steep peaks. We went ashore there. My strength was about to give out completely. There surely could be no Indians in the area because the mountains fell too abruptly. This meant it was safe to light a fire. Melgarejo started one. I had set out all my papers to dry. Some of them ignited but I was too exhausted so I let them burn.

The first day had passed but we were not far enough from the Indians so we hid the raft while we waited out the daylight hours. We had put our ragged clothes out to dry so we were stark naked in the sand. We had lunch and ate the lard. It was February 12. At sundown, we came out of hiding and looked around for logs to rebuild the wrecked raft. We were able to reinforce it by adding four extra logs. We also picked up a few thinner ones for steering. In our ignorance, we thought we would cover a long distance during the night but our hopes faded as soon as we began to float. In the deep of night, our raft swept past rocks at breakneck speed. For a while, the roaring waters drowned all other sounds. Speechless, we raced under a rocky overhang, our submerged logs barely making it through the narrow opening. The current pulled us toward the rocks and moments later we cast a makeshift anchor to keep from going adrift.

The basalt cliffs along the banks of the Limay jut up from soft sedimentary deposits that the water has eroded away forming lava cornices. I thought I had discovered a new phenomenon. It was indeed validated later on by Colonel Obligado, Lieutenant O'Connor, and my partner Moysés, the steersman on the expedition aboard the "Vigilante."

When we emerged from those rocks, we "woke up" to find ourselves in the middle of the river, but that didn't mean our ordeal was over. We were now confronted with other obstacles, for example a submerged island where we were caught in a tangle of tree branches. Precious time was lost. After staring at our own demise in the face several times, we beached on an island and decided not to push our luck that night.

We rested against a trunk at the beach, drying ourselves in the sun until 3 o'clock in the afternoon of the 13th. When we set out again on our voyage, the river was unencumbered by rocks or reefs. Instead, we were faced with more pools of still water than ever before. We lost two hours as we placidly watched the leaves drifting with the current along a spiraling path. In shallow areas, we were forced to tow the raft. Therefore, we had to walk barefoot on the rocks hurting ourselves badly. We spent the night in the tall grasses on the right bank eating sardines from a can and wasting not a single drop of oil.

The weather was mild and the river was increasingly clear, although the pools of still water and the shallow sandbanks –where the raft's speed increased significantly–posed their own share of danger. On the 14th we gained a lot of ground and were thrilled to find that the "Pirquin-Puramue" path was deserted. The trail to Valcheta crosses this path. There were four rafts and fresh tracks, a sign that the Indians had been there and were on our trail. In this remote area the river narrows and becomes extremely picturesque. When I visited the Rhine much later, I was reminded of this volcanic region. Now we were picking up speed around the bends and at one point the raft overturned. Luckily we managed to save it. The incident left us tired and ravenous so we fell asleep on the beach.

At noon on the 15th, we arrived at the location where the Río Negro diverts from the Limay and makes its way into the mountains. We would soon find out whether the much feared messenger had returned and if Antonio had delivered my warning to Colonel Vintter. We looked for telltale signs and found them in what seemed to be the hoof prints of two mounted beasts. What could have happened to them? Our strength had waned, but we continued navigating the river from dawn to dusk. We had not eaten and could not dry ourselves because any fire would have betrayed our presence. The night of the 15th was awful. We had eaten the last of the sardines the previous night and only had the "pâté de foie gras" left, so we fasted. We spent hours on end watching a poor skinny dog that was lost in the barren landscape and did not seem interested in us. We had no fire; there was no chance for a decent piece of meat! I reminisced about passing through the purple fields of "Cum-lelfen" in 1876 and the tired-out mares we abandoned there.

We were hoping to reach the Manzana-Geyú area on the 16th. We were full of anticipation for the big tree, which would be bearing fruit by then. However, when we got there the current was so swift we could not stop. We devoured the green bunches with our eyes alone as we passed by. Nevertheless, we did not dwell on our yearnings because suddenly a thick smoke cloud appeared in the distance, downstream towards Neuquén. Would it turn out to be Christians or Indians out there? Gavino and Melgarejo wanted to signal them with the few matches I was saving in waterproof wrappers from "Rigollot" mustard plasters. However, I knew the Indians were crafty and it occurred to me they might be trying to lure us. Therefore, instead of responding to the smoke, we rode the waters silently through the beautiful red gorges that once fascinated Villarino. At dusk, we arrived at the place where we had seen the smoke. We hid the raft nearby in the dry bed of the "Río del Norte," Picunleufú, and looked for tracks. We counted fourteen fresh marks. The Indians had left the site a few hours before through the mountain path while we traversed the risky waters. That afternoon we celebrated by eating the pâté. We had nothing else edible left. Nevertheless, we kept our spirits up.

The 17th was a gloomy day. We were extremely tired and hungry and had nothing to eat except for some roots. Although there was no shortage of water, our thirst was unquenchable because we had come down with a devastating case of fever. That night we fell completely silent. As we lay on the beach carefully watching the raft that swayed to the smallest current, we began to lose faith in our prospects. Would we make it to Neuquén? Would we find a fort there? We were plagued with doubt.

At dawn on the 18th, we made a final effort to start again. By noon, we could not lift our arms anymore. Unable to steer the raft, we had to abandon it. I was the only one familiar with this isolated area. Neither Melgarejo nor Gavino had traversed it before and it took a lot of persuading before they understood that Neuquén was not far away, and that the lowlands one could see along the eastern horizon were actually the Río Negro. I asked them to follow me on foot. Equipped with a lasso and wearing the leather sandals we had made from Gavino's saddle, we stepped onto solid ground seeking the good fortune denied to us in the water. Moments later we found an Indian trail and my men realized I hadn't tricked them.

I led the way, followed by Melgarejo several meters behind and Gavino, who wasn't much of a walker. It was a pitiful sight. Three starving men walking, falling, and desperately quenching their thirst with water that was not fit for drinking. Drink we did, though, every time we stumbled upon a puddle. In one of those waterholes, I lost consciousness and lay amid the reeds for a long time. A light afternoon breeze blew and I recovered. I realized then that I was on the right path. Ahead we could see the steep, rugged rock that rises above the others to form the northwest corner of Patagonia. I lit a match and set the brush on fire. How could anyone in the adjacent valley fail to see the smoke? If stationed nearby, soldiers would surely come to our rescue. We had no energy left and could not go on any more.

We marched on slowly until the day turned into night. At

this point, we reached a stream that descended from the west, a branch of the Neuquén that empties into the Limay, ultimately feeding into the Río Negro. I asked my men to be brave for one more hour but they weren't listening.

"We are not walking any further, chief. We just can't."

Despite the good prospects of finding food nearby, I decided to wait until the following day.

It was such a hard night among the thorny bushes! My men were so tired they could not sleep. They looked deadly. I, on the other hand, could not become reconciled to the idea of dying when we were so close to being rescued. I had gone through thick and thin. I had made important discoveries. The thousands of leagues once thought to be barren had turned out to be fertile land; the lake was no longer a mystery; the river was navigable. There were no waterfalls to be afraid of, as I had maintained all along despite people's insistence to the contrary.

I set out in search of juicy branches, "cow's tongue" stems, but all I found was a bunch of thorny pods from a tree that looked like carob but was not. The thorns gave me a bloody lip.

When the rising sun painted the sky in shades of red I summoned my companions. I wanted to show them the dark water running from the west as always. It was from the Neuquén. They got up and silently followed me. Two very old wheel ruts proved we were at the merging point between two rivers. Colonel Guerrico had been through here with his carriage. Encouraged by our findings and while the skyline took on differing shades of black and red we climbed up the hill until we reached the end of the road. The Neuquén flows along the foot of this hill. I had traversed this area in 1876. The river ran smoothly and in the sleepy northern valley all was quiet except for a strange dark shape that seemed out of place. Would it be a small fort? As the light of day broke through we saw a cloud of dust, a sign of human life. Would it turn out to be a fort or was a group departing now that the sun had come out?

I took out the flag from under my jacket and had Gavino wave it from the top of the hill while I simultaneously fired my revolver. The shots reverberated back to us. Through the dust cloud we saw people running in all directions. This got our hopes up. After I had fired fourteen shots, a group of veteran soldiers came marching through the forest in a flash. Preparing themselves for battle from the opposite bank, they were astounded when they saw the fluttering flag instead of a bunch of Indian warriors.

One of them waded across the river as far as his horse could touch bottom and shouted:

"Who's out there?"

"Moreno! I escaped from the Indian huts!" I answered.

We were safe. Since we were on the verge of collapse I enlisted their escort across the river. We were naked, and made it across by holding on to our horses' tails. The fort commander, the brave lieutenant, who later became Captain Crouzeilles and was brutally murdered by the Indians in Lonquinay, stepped into the water to welcome me. Lieutenant Batalla, the good old man, offered me a cigar the moment I stepped out of the water.

"I don't smoke, my friend, but I'll take a biscuit if you have it." As I entered the fort, a pair of captive Indians from Shaihueque's camp arrived. Colonel Vintter had sent them with orders to Shaihueque that I be released. Failure to do so would result in his coming down to get me himself. This would not be necessary now. Moreover, I could use the Indians' horses for my journey to Fort Roca.

It would be an understatement to say that the good soldiers had so little, and yet generously offered it to me. The mare broth and twelve biscuits I had were a real treat!

With or without us the fort would have been abandoned by the afternoon. The troops were under orders to retreat to Choele-Choel. Had we arrived a few hours later, we would have perished.

I could not feel my wounds, which had festered in the sun and by contact with the water. Galloping non-stop I arrived at Fort Roca by dusk. I ran into Antonio first. He immediately notified Vintter, who, moments later, helped me get off my horse in front of his house.[37]

All the suffering I had endured between the night of the 11th and that morning was soon forgotten. On the 19th I embraced the new day. I had no desire to rest. A messenger was already on his way to Bahía Blanca with news of my safe arrival. I would soon follow him.

The imprisoned Indians were there. When they heard the news they thought Shaihueque had set me free. However, when the colonel ordered them to march past me and they were able to see the condition of my legs, all their hopes faded. They realized they would never get to see the huts again.[38]

As I had predicted, Shaihueque was imprisoned in Caleufú and five years later was brought to Buenos Aires.

The reader who has come this far will notice an element of noble-mindedness in the savages' behavior. None of the Caleufú chiefs tainted their hands with blood from defenseless captives and none committed murder on the frontier. When they took arms, they were only fighting to keep their territory. On the other hand, the Indians from the Pampas, the plundering Caciques who pillaged their way through the desert, were hostile intruders. Shaihueque, as the master of the land, "the Great Mind," used to say in council that "by God's will they had been born on the other side of the great mountain range," and that his Mapuche ancestors were the sole owners of "the wildlife and the pastureland and the silver from the mountains."

---

[37] Telegram from General Lorenzo Wintter to General Luis María Campos regarding Moreno's escape from Shaihueque's camp. (See Appendix).

[38] This last version of Moreno's reminiscences was published in part by the Diario de Buenos Aires (1885) when the National Armed Forces brought Cacique Shaihueque to justice. The Editorial board of the newspaper stated, "The missing witness will soon come forth and Shaihueque will be able to tell the disbelievers about the courage, cleverness, and cold-bloodedness that Moreno needed to achieve his goal.

As far as I am concerned, I can safely say that whether in freedom or in captivity, Shaihueque never let any one lay his hand on me. I took a stand and he understood. We may have clashed bitterly or argued harshly during the Councils. The warriors' threats may have sounded fierce. However, there was always a measure of respect for white men, whom the Caciques considered rulers just like them. The moral environment in which I was living caused my suffering. I do not blame the Cacique who welcomed me in his hut one day. In 1880, Shaihueque was a loyal foe, and he judged the purebred Indian using Indian criteria. He defended his homeland. He believed he owned the land by divine right.

The following day I traveled to Choele-Choel, and in Chichinal I learned that Bovio was at camp. We had all made it back alive! When I saw my brave friend I gave him a big hug. Sick and worn out, he had walked non-stop from the Tecka huts, where he was handed the letter Utrac had delivered. His clothes tattered, he had come this far to seek assistance for me.[39]

I asked him about our "Vigilante." Before resuming the work I had been commissioned to do, I had to travel to Buenos Aires to report on the investigations completed in the Andean region. It was important at this time given the ongoing talks with Chile regarding the boundary line. Consequently, I had decided that for the time being, Bovio would continue where I had left off.

"I heard some bad news," he told me. "It seems the government is disappointed with you."

Fernandez Oro, who was lieutenant colonel at the time and who received us as guests at his ranch, added:

"You've been dismissed."

"And for what reason?"

"Apparently you have not fulfilled your duties…"

What was going on? I was sure I had carried out my

---

[39] Telegram Moreno sent to his father from Choele Choel (See Appendix).

instructions. What instructions could they be referring to now? The ones in the luggage recovered by Bovio? The ones I had complied with at the risk of losing my life? No, those did not count! The non-existent ones did. They instructed me to limit my scope to a guano-looting prevention effort along the Patagonian coast!

This was obviously a mean-spirited attempt by subordinates at the Ministry to create confusion among their superiors by presenting them with Commander Laserre's instructions as if they had been intended for me. Laserre was in charge of the "Uruguay" expedition.

I hurried back home so I could take care of this matter. The journey by carriage had a detrimental effect on my legs, so much so that at one point between Choele-Choel and Conesa I decided to continue on horseback. I dashed off, galloping steadily until I arrived in Carmen de Patagones by myself on the 29th.[40]

It was lunchtime. The sun beat down on the unpaved, deserted, and sandy street. I called at the grocery store, where I hoped to find friends and get a news update. Shocked by my shabby appearance, someone tried to bar my entrance. I introduced myself and pushed the dining room door open. Thirteen people were standing around the table. Always the same fateful number! They were waiting for the 14th, who turned out to be no other than the 13th participant from back in November!

I received conflicting reports there. Yes, I had been fired; no, I had not been fired. Minister B. Zorrilla was hard put to find a solution to the problem regarding the disappearance or misplacement of the actual instructions. In order to keep my job with the Exploratory Commission Administration I had to obey the missing instructions. As if I had ever disobeyed them in the first place! What nonsense!

If our work had proceeded as planned, it would have prevented many useless arguments. Settlers would have been

---

[40] Letter from his father. (See Appendix).

drawn to this land of plenty and cultivated its fertile soil. Sad to say, there was no development. Not even the Indians live there today! While the "Vigilante" surveyed the Atlantic coast along the Gulf of San Matías looking for harbors, we traversed the territory to the west, getting to know the area, and ascertaining its habitability. We were so engrossed that we reached the Andes and the grassland behind the arid coastline. We were driven by the need to serve our country and did not stop to think of the dangers we were facing. We knew of the difficulties that would plague the setting of boundaries if they were not properly marked. A survey of the Andes was indispensable, together with an analysis of any possible ramifications. We had discovered extensive territories that could be put to good use. My dream was to continue to explore the vast Patagonian territory in this way. However, the Indian lances shining in the moonlight at my campsite in Nahuel Huapi had got in the way of my plans.

I headed back to Buenos Aires by land. I got home exactly a month after my departure from the Caleufú settlement. My physical and emotional health had seriously deteriorated. The situation at the Ministry was an uninspiring and chaotic combination of deceit, inconsistencies, weakness, and lack of concern for my objectives. A copy of the instructions I had been given was nowhere to be found, but it was taken for granted that it would never have included approval for my trip to the Cordillera. Absent from the equation was the fact that the "Vigilante" had not found enough of the promised coal or provisions along the Río Negro to reach its destination. In the opinion of many, the lives of many people aboard the ship would have been lost if we had pushed forward.

The president of the Republic lauded my explorations and, in writing, promised increased support. Nonetheless, the Ministry not only frowned on my work but also relieved me from my duty. I managed to help Dr. Zorrilla save face, but I first made it clear that my actions were without reproach. I tendered my resignation without exposing those who had caused it to public humiliation. I cited health reasons for my decision, confirmed by medical examinations signed by Doctors Rawson, B. Herrera Vegas, Pirovano, and Carlos Lanús, to name a few. I only mentioned the deceased.

After my resignation was accepted, I left for Europe. I needed to regain my physical and emotional strength to resume the struggle for the fulfillment of my ideals.

Early in 1883, almost two years after Moreno's return from Europe, a series of letters was printed in La Nación newspaper regarding Moreno's second expedition to the Cordillera and Lake Nahuel Huapi. Moreno wrote these letters from Córdoba to Lieutenant General Bartolomé Mitre. In them he described his impressions of the trip once again. His first report, sent to Minister Zorrilla, had never been published (see Appendix).

Two years later in Buenos Aires, Moreno ran into the chiefs who had taken him to trial in Caleufú. The "government" had imprisoned the chiefs just as Moreno had forecast during his stay at Shaihueque's huts. He bore no grudge against them, however. What's more, he sought to vindicate them by publishing an article in El Diario de Buenos Aires, which is also an epilogue to his pilgrimage through the wilderness.

El Diario, Buenos Aires.

INACAYAL AND FOYEL

"They stayed over there, on the other side of the river," (namely the Limay, four hundred leagues from this city), Shaihueque answered when I asked him where the above mentioned caciques were. To my astonishment, that afternoon, as I drove a distinguished visitor to Palermo, I got word that Inacayal and Foyel had requested my presence at the barracks of the eighth regiment.

It is a fact that nothing causes more pain during times of duress than the memory of good times past. It is also true that there is some value in reminiscing about the bad times once the good times are back. It is in such happy circumstances that I look back today upon the time I spent at paseo del Parque visiting my old desert friends.

Seeing Inacayal and Foyel in Palermo clashed with my mental image of them in a very different milieu. It also made me think of others who came before and who epitomize the birth of humanity. They were creatures cast adrift in the darkness; they dressed in animal skins, and were surrounded by half-naked, wretched and uncouth females. They were our predecessors. They hailed from the harsh, previous geological era; their fur garments a prosaic first stage in the evolution of clothing. At the paseo, though, the men's elegant garments brought out the beauty we have come to admire. The young Indian women at the barracks lamenting the loss of their huts also evoked the simple beauty of yore.

When I visited Shaihueque at Retiro I was struck by the vivid memories etched in my mind of my terrible experiences at Caleufú and Quem-quem-treu, where I suffered hunger and looked at death in the face. Nevertheless, when I entered the small room containing what was left of the tribe whose company I had once shared, all I felt was sadness. It looked like a shoddy imitation of an Indian camp scene after an orgy. Guanaco hides and dirty Araucanian blankets were lying around in shreds. The unique smell of Tecka was in the air. The tanned, naked chests, the disheveled hair, did not belong in Buenos Aires.

In the dim light of the room I could see the men on one side, the women on the other. Inacayal was lying down. A crouching Foyel, his head tilted to one side, had lost the fierce countenance that once earned him a reputation as a brave warrior. They were disheartened and failed to recognize me at first. Seconds later, they both rose at the same time and greeted me by name. "Moreno!" smiling as they reached out with their right hand. The witness had finally arrived who would say, "They're not bad Indians." Indeed, they were not, a fact of which they knew I was aware.

I will not try to reproduce what they were saying in Araucan or what was being interpreted so poorly. Indians see things differently than civilized men. They cannot stand being in custody. They are not prisoners of war; they have never stolen anything, and they have always shown up when requested to do so. "What will become

*of us?" "Why are they keeping us separated?" It is hard to make
them understand that they are not in danger and that their women
and children will not be taken away from them. Commander García
had assured them of that and they must believe him. However, the
Indians could not forget that, before arriving at the barracks, children would disappear from the crowd of prisoners in the middle of
the night. It is hard to believe in the Christians when the Christians
act that way.*

*In the huts, when the Indians complained about the way white
men treated imprisoned Indian children, I often felt compelled to
admit that they were right.*

*Shaihueque was surrounded by very few of my acquaintances.
However, most of my good friends from the Cordillera were at the
barracks of the eighth regiment. They had once fed me and helped my
courageous friend Bovio out during his distressful illness. They had
aided me in exploring Lake Nahuel Huapi's southern bank. On January 1, 1880, I wrote an official report while at an enclave of huts in
the fertile Tecka plain, by one of the Chubut's tributaries. This area,
surrounded by snow-capped, unnamed mountains and forests, was
home to Inacayal. I named it after Rivadavia. The report, which has
yet to be published, told the nation that a rich expanse of land exist-
ed that was once thought to be all desert. My assertion was confirmed years later by General Villegas and subsequently by Commander Roca. The Indians at the barracks of the eighth regiment
were the ones who delivered this report to Patagones.*

*Not even one among them has been treacherous towards whites,
and those who were, acted in this manner during a legitimate fight
for self-preservation. Today I saw those who used to provide my people with guanaco and ostrich meat every day, the same ones who
warned my people of Mapuche sneak attacks and recommended cau-
tion in my dealings with them. Among the poor women, I recognized those who picked strawberries for Utrac's friend, the white
chief. I enjoyed meeting Inacayal's kind daughter again, the one to
whom I entrusted my shabby suitcase filled with books and papers[41]
before I left for Nahuel Huapi. She took such good care of it that
when she delivered it to an Indian messenger in Viedma a year later
the old thing was intact.*

The half hour I spent with those loyal Indians evoked many memories that flit by me as I write. I could fill many pages of El Diario with these scenes of life in the wilderness. I take pleasure in reminiscing about the discussions on astronomy Bovio and I had on warm January nights at the hut facing east. Our enraptured audience, the primitive men wrapped in quillangos and lying on the ground, listened in awe until they fell asleep, mesmerized by the unimaginable distances and tales from another world. I remember the firework displays and the amazed huiliches trying to fathom the flare in the foothills. In their minds, the brightness was proof that the spirits of the night were obeying our commands, a sign of their unwillingness to cross us during our journey. I also remember the times I was at the "table" with the Indians and managed to do away with the rule of etiquette that forbids women from taking nourishment in front of and at the same time as men.

I wonder if any of the women have been able to forget the sweet taste of quince jelly. I can still see the circle of smiling, pleasantly surprised faces as they licked that tasty red stuff they had at one point mistaken for raw meat. That afternoon, when the young men came home, loaded with ostriches from the hunt, their girlfriends and wives caused a big commotion about the funny meat that tasted better than strawberries. It was quite a racket. I might also mention how men and women alike could scarcely believe their eyes when they saw the portrait collection of my "women friends."[42] Female friendship could only occur among white people; at the huts, women were all slaves. In one corner I ran into the crabby Gennaken who used to spend long hours sitting very still, watching me with piercing eyes, as I wrote the above mentioned report. Then he ran off and I did not see him again until today, when I showed him a sketch of his big, friendly face.

Only a traveler whose experiences matched mine could ever understand how happy I was that day as I looked at the young women and children in the shed. One of them recognized the white

---

[41] Among these, his Ahoneke dictionary where he wrote, in pencil, the rough copy of the report sent to Minister Zorrilla by messenger from Tecka.

[42] Portrait of his sister Maruja, which I still have in my possession. E.V.M

man who had been their guest at the huts. "Moreenu," she said, as
they all rose, drying their tears. They approached in a row to shake
my hand. Today Inacayal still says, "I treat him as if he were my
own son."
    The poor Indians think I count for something. If only it were so,
I would use my valuable influence to obtain their release. I would
have them sent back south. There, instead of living like animals,
leading a life of vagrancy in the infancy of society, fatalistically and
obliviously convinced that, "God had not taught them the ways of
work," they could possibly sow the seeds of future cities. Aware of
his ethnic group's ineptitude for work, Inacayal, who has come up
in the world thanks to his own efforts, has already taken steps in the
right direction. This clever Indian visited Buenos Aires years ago
and brought back new progressive ideas to the village, as suggested
by Mariano D. Baudrix, the kind "laustra huentru" (short, small
man), whom the Indians still remember. Inacayal also put workers
from Valdivia in charge of crop farming in Nahuel Huapi. He also
founded the first Andean center. The city that will someday be built
on the shores of the Great Lake will be situated in the same place
where those excellent shelters –recreated by La Nación years ago–
were built, and where I lived from January 18 to 22, 1880. The
herbal collection at the La Plata Museum contains barley, pea, potato, and pumpkin specimens harvested there.
    Unfortunately, when the lake was settled white people burned
down these huts. Over the centuries we have behaved just like the
querandíes, Inacayal and Foyel's ancestors, who set Buenos Aires
on fire at a time when it was just a bunch of straw huts. "You can't
judge a book by its cover." Inacayal and Foyel are civilized men,
covered with quillango furs and the pampa sarape. Cox, the
Chilean traveler, agrees with me. As the first man to sail Nahuel
Huapi Lake, he shipwrecked in the Limay rapids. The Indians rescued him from the surging waters. Musters, the great explorer, has
oftentimes given credit to them in his fine travel diary, "At Home
with the Patagonians."
    I am writing these lines after returning from Palermo. There,
among the many views that lift the heart and delight the senses, I
have run into classic examples of this vanishing race, having shared

with them their last few days spent in freedom. Readers of El Diario will thus come to know how a good tribe has met its demise. This scene of high drama will not come before us again. Its protagonists will all be gone.

I repeat, Inacayal and Foyel deserve protection. They should not be mixed up with the likes of Pincen and Namuncurá. They have not murdered people; they have given of their hospitality. We must not let them end up in disgrace like Orkeke's tribe.

Francisco P. Moreno

APPENDIX

PART TWO

LETTER FROM LIEUTENANT GENERAL JULIO A. ROCA TO MORENO

Buenos Aires, November 4, 1879

My Dear Friend,

How nice of you to write from Patagones announcing your departure for Choele-Choel. I'm also thrilled with your other letter from la Guardia Mitre, which will be published with commentary in "La Tribuna" tomorrow.

For one thing, it will be powerful evidence of the navigability of the Río Negro.

The worst part of the river lies between Patagones and that point, yet you negotiate those rough waters as if there was nothing to it. From now on you will encounter no more difficulties until you get to the Limay. Who knows? Maybe this season you will be able to sail these rushing waters for a few leagues. One thing you will need is coal, though.

As head of the scientific and exploratory expedition to Patagonia, you must have been well received by the military line chief in Río Negro. I am not afraid at all for the "Vigilante." It is in expert hands. I regret having ordered small ships from England for purposes of sailing the Río Negro. We could have had the same capability as the "Vigilante" but a smaller keel. Nothing else worth mentioning around here. The Chileans are taking the Peruvian offensive quite seriously. An army of 15,000 men is rumored to have landed between Iquique and Arica. We expect news of one of the battles any time now. Wishing you the best. Your good friend,

JULIO A. ROCA

(Letter received in Carmen de Patagones)

REPORT TO HIS EXCELLENCY THE MINISTER, DOCTOR B. ZORRILLA[43]

Latitude 43° 31' 35" South
Longitude 72° 29' 31" West of Greenwich
Tecka Yaguagujano
Inacayal and Foyel's tents
January 5, 1880

Dear Minister Zorrilla:

I sent Your Excellency a telegram with news of my arrival from my successful travels in Patagonia. Now it is my pleasure and duty to inform you about the general conditions of the territory we covered. Even though the decree dated March 13 stated that my commission should limit its scope to the coastal region, I concluded that our work in exploring this part of the territory would fail to bear fruit unless the region was explored in several directions. In light of what has been written about it and based on my own personal knowledge, I decided the Atlantic coast area could not be put to good use as long as the lands forming the Chubut territory remained uncharted.

Your Excellency knows that travel to Patagonia has been infrequent and that public opinion is not always in favor of settling this area. We would have achieved little if we had only explored the land bordering the Atlantic. The first part of the work I envisioned for the commission encompassed an area from the Río Negro to Chubut that would otherwise have been overlooked by the government in the allocation of resources to settlers. For this reason, as I stated in

---

43 Report sent by Moreno to the Minister, Dr. Zorrilla, on January 5, 1880, from Inacayal's huts in Tecka. He wrote his notes in pencil in the "Ahoneke Notebook Dictionary" he had brought from Buenos Aires. It was found amid the papers and books left in a suitcase entrusted to Inacayal's daughter and then delivered via Indian messenger to Viedma a year after Moreno's escape from Shaihueque's huts. Nothing was missing.

my telegram from Choele-Choel, I ordered the "Vigilante" to hug the coast between Río Negro and the Valdés Peninsula in search of the best harbors. My men were instructed to dig wells where running water was scarce, for instance, in San Antonio and San José. I have a lot of faith in these two geographic areas. Once people get to know them they will recognize how important they are for settlement purposes and for shipping products from the vast Chubut territory. The work was to have taken two months. Meanwhile, Bovio, the engineer, and myself, were to penetrate and explore the western region. As your Excellency can see from this second report, my hopes were well grounded. The area was surrounded by mystery and this was the only reason people thought the territory was nearly useless and that it fared poorly against the better-known regions on the Atlantic coast.

On November 12, Mr. Bovio, two sailors, an Indian by the name of Linares, another Indian from Valdivia, and I left Viedma. The two Indians would serve as guides and interpret for us. We brought along twenty-five horses laden with provisions and gifts. We could only advance four leagues that first day because of the rain and bad road conditions caused by flooding. We stayed in San Javier overnight.

On the 13th our horses practically had to swim across several water-soaked areas —former pastures where herds of cattle used to graze. There we witnessed a sad scene. An injured Indian had been abandoned behind a corral by one of his companions. Since the path that runs along the riverbank was not passable we had to skirt around Colina del Sur. We made only nine leagues headway.

When we arrived at La Guardia Mitre on the 14th, the weather was very bad. Thus, we could not take an astronomical reading of our position. We spent the night of the 15th in Angostura. We ran into Shaihueque's messengers, who had come to do business with us. They carried no rations with them and brought bad news about the state of affairs in the territory we would be exploring. On the 16th I camped out to the west of the second Angostura after visiting the pampa Indian Gavino García, Inacayal's nephew, who agreed to come with us.

On the 16th we arrived at D. Serafín García, a settlement in

LoncoHuaca or Cabeza de Buey (Ox Head), after traveling through wonderful fields fertilized by flooding and suitable for cattle raising. On the spur of the moment, Francisco Hernández, another nephew of Inacayal's, joined us there too. We received alarming news from the tents so I decided to send for more weapons from Viedma.

We spent the 17th and 18th determining our astronomical position by using a sundial. Preparations were made for our march into the desert. Forty mares were selected to provide nourishment during the journey. With Mr. Bovio in charge of leading the expedition to the slope of Cashtrú, I was able to cross the river at Guardia Conesa on the 19th and head for Choele-Choel. I had traveled in the region in years past and wished to visit it again now that it had been settled. There I would get a graphic account of the nine men murdered by southern Indians, which would increase my anxiety regarding the future.

I spent the night of the 20th at Fortín Negro Muerto ("The Fort of the Dead Black Man"). My host was Lieutenant Napoleón Narecondo. On the afternoon of the 21st, after galloping across a lush valley for an hour, I arrived at camp. I remained there with Colonel Villegas until the 24th. After I gathered the specific information I needed and added two soldiers to reinforce our escort team, I traveled across the island.

On the 25th I retreated, heading east and arriving in Cashtrú that afternoon. Mr. Bovio and Gavino were waiting for me. Hernández got there at the same time, as did the messenger sent to Viedma to pick up our order. Our group of six men had grown into a party of 16. Eleven were armed. This spot, at a longitude 65° 37' 39" west of Greenwich, was to be our entryway. On the night of the 27th, we headed West Southwest on the compass under the light of the moon. At 12 midnight, we camped out on the mesa at some distance from the Kala-Gueta hill. Luck was with us. We found water in a lagoon where, normally at this time of year, there should have been none. It rained for a long time that day.

On the 28th we walked all day. We labored across the Walichu basin, a deep, waterless canyon in a desolate area of uninviting, thorny shrubs and dunes. Terror increases the superstitions of the Indians. In one of the hollows in the tertiary rock alongside the road, we found some offerings they had made to the Eternal Spirit as a supplication not to be attacked by thirst, and for their horses not to tire in this dreaded ravine that had claimed more than a few innocent lives.

After walking the whole day, we camped out on the basin's Southern plateau, where there was still no water to be found. On the 29th, we set off at dawn. After going down a series of hills, we got to Valcheta valley. By noon we were drinking water from a brook and had camped out on its banks at the entrance to a narrow pass. There were no tertiary rocks here, though.

Between Cashtrú and Valcheta there were good, strong grasses everywhere except for the Walichu Basin. If the area were irrigated on a regular basis, cattle could certainly graze here but this would require man's intervention. On the foothills that rose from the plateau that separated Walichu from Valcheta and at the entrance to the basin there was a salt plain. It was a good source of common salt for the Indians and was located next to the path that travels through Nahuel-geyú and across Huincul-Mapu until it reaches the west southwestern end of Valcheta on the Limay River.

The grassy Valcheta valley, located on the lower part of the plateau, got a lot of rain in winter, I noticed. The water reaches the road and then in the summer retreats towards the Indian area of Longelú. Sodium sulfate abounds; still, there is much land that is suitable for agriculture, and, in general, for cattle raising. The stream that runs from the southwest through the narrow passage is never dry.

We remained there until December 1 in the afternoon. Our horses needed to rest, and we had specimens as well as observations to collect. We saw several graves or Indian cairns crowning the peaks. We headed west along the edge of the Valcheta valley. It was a struggle because the lowlands were soaked and wild grasses grew in abundance. We crossed a small stream whose name I do not remember, and spent the night beside a fork in the stream that forms a lovely islet amid mountains and mesas. The water from the streams could easily be used for irrigation since the slopes are very steep. The climate is cold and rainy, with frequent showers.

Early on the second, we left the stream behind and headed west southwest through a broad, sandy, nitrate-rich mountain pass. Many of the tertiary formations that lined the path had large lava stains. We arrived at Yaquépajetran, a salt-water stream that runs along a south-north axis over plutonic rock and then empties into the Nahuel-Geyú at Valcheta. There is only a tiny Indian outpost that the natives have visited frequently for many years. We picked up many stone arrowheads, just as at the previous camp.

On the 3rd. we arrived in Treneta, a fine camp featuring springs and encircled by medium and low hills, their verdant slopes desirable for cattle raising. Some of these areas seemed fit for agriculture as well. Along the way there was a lake containing a plentiful supply of sodium chloride (common salt). The temperature was mild. At 9 a.m. it was 4° C, and at 5 p.m. it was 16° C.

On the fourth, we continued west. We scaled and descended three rugged basalt ranges. These rock-studded slopes were separated by three basins approximately 150 meters deep (according to the barometer). These valleys were Indian gathering places: Yem-Neu, Iquen-Alept, and Famuelen. We camped in Famuelen, the largest of the three. It is extremely fertile and has great settlement potential. There was a permanent water source there as well as plenty of grassland in the surrounding area.

On the fifth, we were stranded due to bad weather. Besides, our horses needed to rest. We headed west again on the sixth, through lowlands covered with grass and surrounded by lava rock. It was a cold, rainy day. Fresh running water was scarce around there but easily obtainable by digging small holes. We passed Yaguepa-Ateck and Yaguipagetran, and then descended towards a huge valley dominated by black basalt rocks on its southern border. To the north the beautiful Janguisketan ridge and its tertiary formations –I am not sure of some of these names– were the prominent feature.

We camped in K'gicha, an area fit for development and colonization. On the seventh, we left behind us to the north the road used by Musters, which leads to a place whose name starts with an "M." We experienced the backcountry in its entire splendor as we traversed gently rolling hills. At noon we arrived at Yagagton, where a high basalt mesa borders the valley. That afternoon we scaled this rocky plateau 160 meters above the valley. We trudged across the broken mass of lava rock, which is utterly devoid of sand or earth. Nothing softened the jagged-edged fragments we encountered. Our horses had an extremely difficult time. From our vantage point we could see a lagoon that lay permanently hidden twenty meters down below, between the vertical basalt walls of a twenty-meter deep gorge. Some of the high elevations to the south and northwest were covered with snow. The large shrubs had all but disappeared from sight, giving way to a profusion of small plants with beautiful flowers.

On the eighth at 5AM, it was 1° C below zero [30° F]. We climbed a mountain a short distance away towards the southeast. It is an extinct crater, the caldera of an ancient volcano. Like others here, it used to spew lava across hundreds of leagues. The centuries-old lava cooled off but its remnants retained certain characteristics. The crater is twelve meters deep, sixty in diameter, and is covered with grass and pretty flowers (blooming calceolarias). It rises approximately 220 meters above Yagagton Valley.

We continued south across the cooled off lava, leaving behind a volcanic peak to the north. We proceeded down the slopes through basalt gorges and tertiary formations until we reached Yamnagoó plain. We camped at Sheile, located at 41° 46' and 68° 26' 15," a vast flatland which boasted an abundance of water. The Ap'pa and Dalaguepu range bordered it on the south and southwest. I believe settlers will be drawn to this rich land the Indians often visit and will one day establish thriving populations.

We arrived a few days after the Indians abandoned the area following the death of a young man there. The decomposed bodies of the recently sacrificed dead animals were scattered about. We stayed there until the 11th. Judging by our observations, the Indians could not be too far off and were probably watching us. Their smoke signals, responding to our own, crowned the mountains nearby.

We took off, heading south-southwest. Before long we ran into Cacique Puitchualao's tents. We were well received and remained at this Gennaken camp until the 13th. Then we resumed our journey going west through valleys, broad and narrow, swan lakes, and the ever-present mountains that surrounded them. Hundreds of guanacos driven off the lowlands by hunters and their bolas were searching for their next meal among the abundant grasses.

We traversed mountain ridges measuring about 1000 meters in height above sea level, according to barometric measurements. Crystalline spring waters were streaming down the mountain. We went down to a fertile meadow and worked our way to Yatunsk-Taje, where we set up camp for the night. All day we had been marching through a succession of fields highly suitable for cattle farming and in some places even for agriculture. The country was broken by gulches, valleys and prairies. There was one path leading towards the Chubut Colony. We did not dare cross the deep-running waters of a stream that flowed out of an area called "Yaly" or something like that. Instead, we took the surrounding overland trail.

On the 14th we crested a narrow but fertile gorge carved into a lava layer 200 feet thick. Inside the crack we found several caves, the ancient dwellings of the region's primitive settlers, whose lifestyle was similar to that of the old world inhabitants of the Stone Age and the glacial era. I assigned a group of people to dig there while I headed off to the much-celebrated Mackinchau or Maquinchao plain. Mr. Bovio was left in charge of ascertaining our location astronomically.

The region is deservedly famous among the Indians. I believe it is bound to achieve prosperity. It is a magnificent piece of land irrigated by the stream that rises in Yalumpe-Lagon and washes more than a thirty-league stretch. Other streams, lagoons, and springs enrich the soil there.

Eyeing the high hills to the west, we took a different trail across a grassy area. After galloping all day we got to a place called Maicktr or something, where I met Mr. Bovio. He had been unable to carry out his astronomical observations due to foul weather, but largely the excavation had been fruitful.

On the 15th we continued to explore the caves. I was lucky. We dug out a sizable collection of human remains and some weapons. I was also able to copy the painted figures on the rock. Two Indians came by and corroborated, in part, the news brought by Puitchualao or Pichuala. The Picunches were getting hungry. On the 16th we *left the beautiful Maicktr prarie and ventured into the fertile central mountain region, where grass, springs, and creeks abound. We spent the night near an ancient Indian cave.*

On the 17th we scaled a peak I estimated to be 1200 meters above sea level in an area of even higher elevations. Then we initiated our descent to the cave. The Andean divide runs through here. One watercourse runs east through Maicktr —I do not know if I am spelling this correctly— and the other flows west. We followed the latter. The whole region is well suited for colonization. We camped in Calgadept something or other, at 42° 10' 51" latitude and 70° 32' 16" longitude. It was a spot blessed with excellent drinking water. It snowed all day.

We set off early on the 18th. The whole day we traversed lush valleys surrounded by mountains. The Andes stood guard in the distance. That night we camped out beside a salt-water lake fed by sulfurous springs. It had been two months since our departure from Buenos Aires.

Early on the 19th we set up camp by a spring located a short distance from the southwestern edge of the lake. Our horses were exhausted from the march. The land along this route is good and all of it is useful. On the 20th I noticed the ground tapers down from Calgadept. After traveling through a valley with dense grass and crossing canyons that slice into the plateau we found ourselves in another valley dominated by tertiary mesas. Initially mountainous it then gave way to a beautiful grassy meadow. We stepped over chunks of volcanic rock and camped near the first of the northern tributaries of the Chubut river. Flooding had ravaged this Indian outpost but we found relief under the shade of the willows. It was a very hot day. In the afternoon we muddled through marshy ground until we reached a plateau that stretched north-northwest towards Nahuel Huapi. We spent the night near another tributary, which ran through a valley that was narrower and more fertile than the first.

On the 21st we treaded across an extremely dense grassy clearing, rimmed by high but nonetheless very fertile hills. Judging by the scattered boulders, some of them ten square meters in size, I concluded it must have undoubtedly been an ancient windswept

*moraine. In the afternoon we arrived at Queluya G. Valley and
indulged in the beautiful views.*

*There, through groves of pepper trees, runs the main tributary of
the three that connect with the Chubut River in the north. It is an
extremely lush river valley, with superb views of meadows speckled
with calceolaria plants, snow-capped mountains to the west, and a
forest that drapes the foothills.*

*On the 22nd I sent messengers north and south to search for
Indians. Our horses were in bad shape and needed to rest. The
weather was cold and rainy. This year appears to be exceptional for
it has rained and snowed much more than in previous years. On the
23rd I clambered up the adjacent slope to 400 meters above the valley. However, the appearance of sharp-edged rocks stopped me from
going any further. The view from this point inspired nothing short
of awe. Flowers bloomed in soft colors and their perfume was
exquisite. Water cascaded down the craggy hillside, spilling into
ferns and through holes in the rock. The beauty of this much-
maligned Patagonian territory startled me. The messengers arrived
that day with word that Inacayal and Foyel were camping out a few
days' distance to the south. On the 24th we crossed the river and
continued to move due south along the flanks of the picturesque Sil-
big Range that stretched to the west. Musters gave a detailed
description of its poignant color.*

*We set up camp by the tents in Deppa. It is a magnificent site
that will serve future settlers well, complete with an ample supply
of wood for construction, the finest lands, and numerous streams.*

*No walking was done on the 25th. On the 26th we headed south
over hills covered with glacial debris. The ice that once buried this
area under a blanket of crystalline ice now fertilizes the region with
its remnants. Galloping amid clumps of grass was cumbersome, no
matter how splendid the sights, though. The springs' were rimmed
by flowering bulrush whose sharp-edged leaves stood at least half a
meter tall.*

*We crossed four streams that ran among the trees and through a
series of small glens in an area once exposed to the wind. During
this season, the streams empty into the Chubut. Along the way we
ran into an Indian messenger sent by Inacayal, who was waiting in*

Tecka. At noon we camped in a small grove of Antarctic birch trees (Fagus Ant.) in Paradero Esquel in order to make astronomical observations.

In terms of its beauty and colonization potential, I would say this is one of the best spots in Patagonia. Fields stretch across hillsides as far as the eye can see. Forests grow in the rocky flanks of the western range and reach far into the wavy plains. Strawberries thrive around the water's edge.

At two in the afternoon our journey progressed south. We were faced with a vast sea of green that reached the Andes foothills to the west. Someday an Argentine city will be founded there and its dwellers will replace the nomadic Indian tribes.

We proceeded east-southeast because the road south was bad for our exhausted horses. After galloping for a few hours we stopped on the left bank of the Tecka for the night. This river runs southwest and empties into the Chubut. The lower reaches of a two-hundred-foot moraine enfold a fertile valley shaped like a semicircle.

On the 27th we followed this narrow valley towards the tents. The hummus-rich soil under our feet could be devoted to agriculture quite successfully. The adjacent mountains were overgrown with grass. We crossed several brooklets and springs, arriving at Caskell at noon. The Indians had abandoned the place the day before, and were gathered in Teck'a to welcome me. We found shelter from the burning sun under the shade of some pepper trees. It was 25° C [77° F] while we waited for the couriers.

As the march progressed, five Indians came up to us. Led by Utrac, Inacayal's son, they expressed a desire to postpone the solemn welcome ceremony until the following day. It was too late to make conversation so we spent the night beside the stream in a lush, fertile valley 1000 meters from the tents, in plain view of the natives.

In the early morning hours of the 28th, Inacayal let me know he was ready. The Indians were lined up in front of the tent when we got there.

Mr. Minister, please forgive me if I digress to give you a detailed description of this ceremony. One hundred and thirty Indians participated. They were armed with lances, shotguns, carbines, sabers, and large knives (facones). These desert dwellers honored the national flag unfurled in front of the fourteen arriving men. They soon started running around in circles of joy, performing military exercises, shaking hands, and shoving away the Walichu so it would not cause trouble. This gave way to the council meeting in front of the tents. When I addressed their parliament I emphasized to Caciques Inacayal and Foyel and their chieftains Pichacana and Patria that the government looked favorably on those Indians who kept the peace. I explained the reasons for my visit and my hopes of getting assistance from them.

Our camp has been set up there since that day. Our whole purpose, Mr. Minister, has been to use our time productively. I apologize for not writing a more extensive report at this time but I am sure this will serve as proof that the Argentine Republic possesses thousands of leagues of prime land in a region that has long been ignored. The potential for growth and prosperity is there. If the work of the "Vigilante" succeeds, nothing will stand in the way of progress for the vast Chubut territory. After the oceanic coast is known, the rich interior will offset the scarcity of resources.

At Quiluya-Getu we came to a mountain range whose peaks are now covered with snow. I named it "MONTE RIVADAVIA." My goal is to continue to explore this area, where cities with large populations will one day stand. People will honor the name for years to come. It will be a beacon for all future immigrants. Mr. Minister, you will notice the repetition of the words "good land," "fertile soil," etc, but believe me, this report pales in comparison to the amazing reality I am faced with here every day. The territory that is closest to the coast is much less noteworthy than the areas further inland. With the exception of a volcanic area we did not encounter any arid land west of Famelen. I cannot praise these foothills enough. This is not an overstatement.

I have to remain here for a while, at least for a month and a half because our horses are falling apart. I will not be idle, though. By the time you read this letter that I am having delivered via messenger, I will have resumed my explorations. In three or four days I will be leaving for Nahuel Huapi on a borrowed horse. I will reconnoiter the southern and eastern shores of the lake. It is too bad I will *not be able to cross the river. It would not be safe. The unfriendly Manzaneros work for Namuncurá. I will survey the region and will return along the Andean foothills back here or to Esquel at the end of the month. If I can get my hands on a few more horses, I will leave half my people here and venture west into the river on a reconnaissance voyage. Then I will return, and as soon as the messenger comes back, I will head west in order to inspect the pass Musters spoke of, the one with the wild herds. After that I will travel south, to Sengüel or Senguer river, a very important one for my mission. I will follow it to the Chubut. From there I will return to Patagones along the seacoast, with the help of the "Vigilante." I plan to finish this task before March 15 or March 30. By that time I hope to be in Río Negro to conduct my explorations of the Santa Cruz region in good weather.*

The map, as well as the rest of the scientific data obtained during this trip will be delivered to Your Excellency as soon as possible.

For my part, all I want is for the Superior Government to approve of my conduct, if it were so inclined. Let me commend the efforts of my companions, especially Mr. Francisco Bovio, the engineer. I would also request permission to spend a modest sum in rewarding my two guides. Don Hernández and Gavino García, as well as a few others who have voluntarily lent their presence to the task. It is a pleasure to send my greetings to Your Excellency from this distant corner of the Republic.

May God bless you,

FRANCISCO P. MORENO

LETTER DELIVERED TO MORENO
IN NAHUEL HUAPI,
WHEN HE WAS TAKEN PRISONER BY ORDER
OF CACIQUE SHAIHUEQUE

———————

Indian Government of Las Manzanas

Río Caleufú, January 15, 1880

To Don Francisco P. Moreno and my two nephews
Don Francisco Hernándes and Don Gabino N.

My friend and my nephews:

Greetings to you and allow me to express my most sincere appreciation, wishing you a good stay and hoping that you arrived happily at the house of your first cousin Modesto Inacayal. I shall remain here, God willing, entirely at your disposal.

My dearest friend and my nephews, after doing the honors, I am glad to explain the purpose of my Commission provided to you last month through my secretary Loncochino in the company of thirty-five men, to welcome you as you deserve, as my esteemed friends upon hearing that you were on your way to this part of the country. That way, I made sure you would be received well. Now, I am receiving news that you were told that many men are coming for you to finish you off. That report about me is false, very, very false. My friend, ever since we had the pleasure of meeting and shaking hands, I have appreciation for you and for that reason I promised loyalty. I now reaffirm that promise and will do so again. But Moreno, after talking to you as my friend, let me tell you that your godson, Francisco Guilliqueque, my son, is very clever, and rides like a good Gaucho.

But my friend Moreno, my nephews Francisco Hernándes and Gabino N., I tell you frankly that I wish you to come to this land to get news from you. I also want to rejoice in your presence and talk to you in person. I hope you will grant me this ambitious wish.

Favorite amigo and nephews, finally, it is my honor to inform you as follows. I have been told that the reports say it was my men who have been pillaging and robbing wagons from the Choelechel garrison. As for that criminal act, I tell you truly, that it was the northern Indians who pillaged wagons and stole animals and other items. They transported them on the Limay river, in close proximity to my tribes, to avoid responsibility for their intolerable crime. That's why I'm very upset because now we're suspects in that crime. Thank God I have been truly faithful to my promises. As God is my witness, I don't think the Supreme Government of the Nation and the authorities are paying attention to the fact that the Picunche Indians are scheming against me. For that reason I am taking the liberty to inform you of this intolerable crime. I am informing you so you do what you need to do.

May God protect you.

By order of my Superior Government Don Balentín Saygüeque

Signed: *José Antonio Loncochino, Sertrio*[44]

Explanatory note handwritten by Francisco P. Moreno on the same letter:

"Letter handed to me by Loncochino when he took me prisoner in N. Huapi. There were not just 35 men at the time but 60. Others had joined the group after seeing me coming from the south."

Signed: *FRANCISCO P. MORENO*

The letter is addressed to Mr. F. P. Moreno, Mr. Franco Hernández, and Mr. Gavino N.

From Governor BALENTIN SAYGÜEQUE
IN TEGUECHUS TERRITORY

---

[44] José Antonio Loncochino was Cacique Shaihueque's spokesperson and secretary.

MILITARY TELEGRAPH
ARGENTINE REPUBLIC

Mister Moreno (Don Francisco Facundo Moreno). It is my pleasure to deliver to you the following telegram I have just received.

Sincerely,

Luis María Campos[45]

Bahía Blanca, February 25, 1880. 3:20 p.m.

To the Weapons Inspector General, Buenos Aires.

Moreno has just arrived here, having escaped from the Indian encampments and after sailing downriver on a raft for seven days. There has been an Indian uprising. I am keeping the Indians I have. I do not expect the commission I sent will ever be back. They would not let them return now that Moreno has escaped.

My regards to you,

LORENZO WINTHER[46]

General Roca Fort, February 19, 1880

Explanatory note handwritten on the same document by Francisco P. Moreno in pencil and dated July 9, 1903.

This morning when I arrived at the fort I met Colonel Winther's 'commission': three Indian prisoners. They returned to Winther's

---

[45] General Luis María Campos.
[46] General Lorenzo Vintter.

camp with me, arriving one hour after the telegram had been handed to the messenger.

Francisco Facundo Moreno's handwritten copy of the telegram that his son Don Francisco P. Moreno sent to him immediately upon his arrival at Choele-Choel after escaping from Shaihueque's tents.

OFFICIAL – I am rushing to give you the good news you have been waiting to hear. Yesterday afternoon I arrived at this spot after reaching the First Division fort at the confluence of the Limay and Neuquén Rivers in the morning. This territory is the most beautiful I have ever explored, but I have also never had so many things go wrong. The report I wrote to the government from Tecka pales next to the splendid region immediately to the south of Nahuel Huapi. I was not taken captive in battle. Rather, I was the victim of a clever trick. My eagerness to continue exploring a certain part of the territory led me to fall into the trap set by Shaihueque. First the War Junta at Quem-Quem-Treu prosecuted me on the third of this month. Then the medicine man sentenced me. I was to be cut open while still alive, my heart offered to God. Luckily I managed to escape with my companions on the night of the 11th and avoided being slaughtered during a big orgy held on the ninth. When we got to Collón Curá we sailed downstream on the raft we had spent two nights building. We also sailed the Limay. The voyage lasted six days and six nights amid steep drops, currents and countercurrents. On the 18th at four in the afternoon we abandoned the raft that saved us because we could not muster the strength to steer it. We were overwhelmed by exhaustion and hunger. We labored on foot until early yesterday when the first division guards from the fort came to our rescue. I salvaged the flag, my diary, and some instruments, except for the theodolite. It was too heavy to carry. My legs have taken quite a beating. It was a long, arduous walk. I was barefoot; it was hot, and branches and rocks hurt my legs. Tomorrow I am heading off to Patagones. From there I will move on to Buenos Aires to give the government a report of this leg of my journey and of the events taking place in the region where the Indians have rebelled. I am not writing any more because I plan to be there at the same time as the mail. I send a big hug and hope to see you soon. My regards to my brothers and sisters.

FRANCISCO P. MORENO

Choele-Choel, February 20/1880

LETTER FROM HIS FATHER
DON FRANCISCO F. MORENO

———————

March 1, 1880

My Dear Pancho:

General Campos had the courtesy to inform me right away of the contents of Colonel Vinter's telegram. I really appreciate his swift handling of the news of your arrival in Choele-Choel after fleeing from the Indians. I am sure you can understand how relieved we feel now that we know. You can imagine our reaction to the letter you wrote us from your friend's huts under the watchful eye of the infamous Loncochino!

As soon as I was notified I put in a request to the War Minister to expedite delivery of a telegram I wrote explaining to you that we had received news of your escape, that we were all doing fine on this end and were eager to help you with all your needs.

While I was working on this I was immensely pleased to read the telegrams you sent to the War Minister and to the Minister of Foreign Affairs in which you announced you were on your way to Patagones and then on to Buenos Aires. Both were published.

My son, this is the best possible news you could give us. After all your troubles, it would do you good to take some time off to be with family and friends before you venture off on a new and exciting adventure (exciting for you, I mean). Hope to see you soon.

By the way, you are becoming more and more popular in this country every day. Forgive me for emphasizing the word popular. That is just the way your father is.

Yours,[47]

---

[47] Sent by his father to Patagones.

FRAGMENT OF THE SECOND LETTER MORENO SENT TO LIEUTENANT GENERAL BARTOLOMÉ MITRE FROM CÓRDOBA, TELLING HIM ABOUT HIS SECOND EXPEDITION TO THE CORDILLERA AND NAHUEL HUAPI

"LA NACION" 1883

At a late-season social function last winter, a group of marine officers stood out among the fluid silks and gauzes donned by the other guests and the jewels that sparkled throughout the reception room. Colonel Erasmo Obligado and his helpers were saying goodbye that night because they were scheduled to depart on a journey the following day. They were returning to the Limay River in hopes of reaching the famous Nahuel Huapi lake whose waters flow into it. They had already sailed the Limay before and almost made it to the spot made known by Villarino.

I approached the officers and as we started reminiscing about this distant region, we became oblivious to our elegant surroundings, so different from the area that was the focus of our conversation. For them it was largely unfamiliar territory; for me it was not.

On their last expedition they had sailed upriver until they passed the Collón-Curá confluence and had reached the same point I crossed as a prisoner. We talked about that rustic place, the terribly strong currents, and last but not least, of the obstacles encountered by the marines aboard the "Río Negro" steamship. They had faced danger and suffered hardship comparable to what I had gone through two years before when I escaped from the tents of Caleufú on a raft made of willow branches. I gave a thorough description of Nahuel Huapi, which for them was "acqua incognita." I also promised to send more information in writing. But one thing led to another and I have yet to do so, so I will send it now for them to read while they brave the same waters that Villarino's barge and my raft once had to cut through.

It has been three years since my last visit to the lake. During that time, an army unit, fifteen hundred men strong, set up camp there under General Villegas' command. On April 1, 1881, fifteen months after my visit to the area, the colossal Andean range was rumbling with cannon fire while the immaculate white peaks captured the glow of our national colors. However, nobody mentioned that these soldiers were marching in the footsteps of other fellow compatriots who came before. The colors shimmering in the big lake are etched in my memory. These same colors were worn by other Argentines clad in similar army uniforms: two of us in 1876 and six in 1880 who became the first white men to reach the mighty Andean range from the Atlantic, revealing its wealth and pointing the way for the Argentine armies that would come through later on. How could I forget the name of my assistant, Manuel Silva, who arrived at the lake with me on January 22nd, 1876, Celestino Moron (a Viedma police warden), and the marines from the "Vigilante," Antonio Van Titter and Juan Gonzalez, my companions in 1880?

There is no mention of these expeditions in General Villegas' report of his forays to the lake. I understand the reasons for this oversight. They have to do with the fact that my extensive1880 report to the Interior Minister was withheld from public scrutiny. Although its publication had been ordered, it was suppressed just as the account of my official mission to the south of Argentina had been during the previous Administration.

That report proved I had found the entrance to the famous Bariloche Pass, whose location I had suspected from my very first trip. However, while the authorities hushed up my findings, explorers were sent to reconnoiter the "long lost pass." Moreover, when he was seeing Commander Olascoaga off to an area north of Río Agrio, the President of Argentina said about the impending explorations, "We need to find the Bariloche Pass in order to avoid a war between Argentina and Chile."

Circumstances like this one have overshadowed the success of my Nahuel Huapi expeditions. Part of the problem is due to the delay in publication of the numerous observations gathered during the five trips I made to the area. However, the work of compiling all this material is so time-consuming it will take years to unravel. I brought with me all the soil samples that it was possible to trans-

port but I have only been able to publish just a few essays describing them very broadly. I have addressed the soil composition and structure of the lands I visited and turned in the results of my studies and observations to the publisher.

I am sending you a copy of one of my travel sketches for you to publish in "LA NACION." The first building is no palace but rather a humble thatched hut in the middle of the forest. Still, in my dreams I have seen it as the keystone of the New Geneva, a city on our own Leman,[48] even more majestic than its Alpine counterpart. In my official report, I indicated that the region styles itself as "the Switzerland of South America." It has no inhabitants, though.

When the army builds the city, this explorer's dreams will come true. In my third letter I will send a description of the lake.

Transcription of a paragraph from General Villegas' letter regarding my trip, which brings back memories of the kind welcome he gave us in Choele-Choel.

"Is there any doubt in anyone's mind that you have been in Nahuel Huapi twice? I do not think so. I can assure you that I could never have accomplished what you did even with the support of someone who would come to my rescue and save me from danger. I remember your last trip. I embraced you at Choele-Choel camp and said, "Farewell, my friend, you won't be coming back." Luckily I was wrong. It is so nice to have you back so we can reminisce about those beautiful regions. Your friends must be happy to see you."

FRANCISCO P. MORENO

Córdoba, January 14, 1883

---

[48] Lake Nahuel Huapi.

LETTERS FOUND ON PAGES 18/21 OF MORENO'S NOTEBOOK, TESTIMONY TO HIS GOOD FAITH TOWARDS THE INDIANS

La Plata, October 2, 1886

Mr. Marcelino Vargas
Buenos Aires

My Dear Sir:

For your information, Foyel and his representative are leaving for Tigre now. They look happy to me. I got approval from the War Minister for this Cacique and his family –brothers, sisters, and spokespersons, fifteen people in all– to come and live with me at the museum[49] until they are sent back to their settlements. It is all I can do for now, but I cannot seem to get very far because the spokesman does not seem to understand what I tell him and is getting in the way of my travel plans. I fear that when the Minister, Dr. Pellegrini, resigns or departs on the 10th of this month, somebody with whom I have no ties will replace him. Then I will not be able to help the poor Indians I love so much. I want them to come with me as soon as possible. That is why I have sent them some money and a museum employee to help them. However, to ensure the success of my plan I need you to let them know they must obey the museum clerk. Once they are well situated here with me in good rooms and have horses available to them, I will try to improve the situation of the good Indians still remaining in Tigre.

Hoping you will one day visit this city and the museum, I thank you in advance for all your help.

Yours gratefully,

F.P. MORENO

---

[49] The La Plata Museum.

La Plata, October 2, 1886

Mr. Antonio Muratorio,
Tigre Grounds Chief

Dear Sir:

I am sending you the telegram I have just received from the War Minister, Dr. Carlos Pellegrini. It refers to the surrender of Caciques Inacayal and Foyel, their brothers, sisters, wives and children –that is, Inacayal, one brother, his wife, and three or four children, Foyel, his brother, his wife and children, and the spokesperson– a total of fifteen people. A long time ago I was granted a similar request by General Victorica. However, based on the mistaken information I received regarding the whereabouts of these Indians, I did not pursue the matter. I was told they were no longer in Buenos Aires, that they had been sent back to the countryside. I now know that they are still here and I wish for them to be released to me. I want to compensate them for their humane treatment of me during my visit to the Andes in 1880.

To avoid any inconvenience at boarding in Tigre, I am sending you Mr. Telémaco Arvelli, an employee of our museum, who will hand deliver this letter and then spend some time –as much as you deem necessary– collecting natural history samples from the area while you order the transfer of the Indians. I urge you do so as soon as possible.

Thank you for returning Dr. Pellegrini's telegram. Let me know if there is anything I can do from my end.

Yours gratefully,

F. P. MORENO

PART III

YEARS LATER

The explored regions, his vision of the future
of these areas, their natural resources,
and his concern for their development.

YEARS LATER

It has been twenty years since Moreno escaped from Cacique Shaihueque's tents. Upon learning that Lieutenant General Julio A. Roca, who was President of Argentina at the time, was traveling to the southern territories, Moreno wrote to him from London, where he was to give expert testimony before the arbiter. The following is the letter he wrote:

London, June 2, 1899

Mr. Lieutenant General Julio A. Roca:

My Dear Friend and General:

Just yesterday, I sent to Confluencia a telegram for you. I once crossed from Las Flores –the railway started there at the time– to Nahuel Huapi when the area was practically a desert. Now that you have smoothed the way for civilization to take hold I can see my dreams coming true sooner than I anticipated during those long marches across the country. I hope everything else follows suit. We must waste no time. When we celebrate our nation's first centennial, we must introduce this region in the grand manner it deserves. In terms of its physical features, our soil is exceptionally good. We must publicize the fact that it ranks among the best in the world. Moreover, we should settle this land and build the strong communities it was meant to sustain. Those of us who participated in this task and who live to see the day will be thrilled by the sight, and equally thrilled as we realize that our lives have contributed to something worthwhile. You have a vision for the future of this land. There will be setbacks, I am sure, given the present population mix. It will be hard to eradicate deep-rooted weaknesses, to make people understand your intentions are worthy, to persuade them of the need for certain social and political reforms, and to bring together people with similar goals and ideals. Some very industrious indi-

viduals have become part of your government and have a plan of action. That is a rarity nowadays. I think there are good things in store for you despite the morbid pessimism –often fueled by the opposition– that predominates among many of our fellow-countrymen. I am an avid follower of Agustín Alvarez of "Tribuna." If you have the chance, please congratulate him for me.

On Monday I made a presentation at the Royal Geographic Society. I am satisfied with the outcome. Major Darwin, Charles Darwin's son and Honorary Secretary of the Society, read from the text in which I had quoted his father several times. At the forum, I pointed out the highlights of a series of 65 fabulous photographic slides. I think my lecture must have made a good impression on the Argentines in attendance. We should send a message to the world that our country has a lot to offer. Since we have not achieved the stature we deserve as an American nation, it is our duty to promote ourselves.

As soon as I have the transcript of the lecture I will forward it to you. I am just sending you the excerpt regarding the present government's objectives which won a lot of praise, as well as the final segment which refers to the British Scientific Societies' proposal to send scholars to do research into some of the issues I referred to in my speech. I think it would be advantageous for us to have the unprejudiced support of these competent men of science at this time. Once we make ourselves known, we will be held in much higher esteem, General.

We must have confidence in our goals and gain the recognition due to us. Based on the first-hand knowledge I have of the rich soil of our beloved country, I strongly believe in its high economic· potential. Moreover, I want the world to value and appreciate its resources. The goals of your administration will be greatly enhanced by the great men of science who will visit us. What seems like an insurmountable task to some, will probably turn out to be quite easy to accomplish and highly productive. We need to compare differences and similarities and yet we neglect to do so. We talk about arid lands, deserts, difficulties in communication, etc., but we fail to see that other countries have managed to rise from even poorer conditions and achieved greatness in the process. I need not be a visionary to see that people will flock to the now water-scarce inte-

rior provinces once irrigation systems that utilize the heavy sea-
sonal rainfall are put into place and our rich local mineral reserves
are mined. As far as the Patagonian territories, extraordinary
things could be accomplished there.

I think we have enough coal reserves in our country and their
condition is good but we need adequate studies and the encouragement of unprejudiced men of science to carry them out. The Argentine government has lent effective support to many scientific explorations. I need only mention Lieutenant Bore's, Dr. Nordenskjold's
and, most recently, "Belgium," but none have been as important as
the one that is underway now under my direction. I am sure you
will work within the system in order to contribute to the success of
our operation. Easing the problems of transportation and providing
effective recommendations for the altruistic men who come here to
work would be a good start.

I just saw our friend De Martino. He was in the process of paint-
ing his last canvas on the Trafalgar epic: the British fleet led by the
"Victory" the morning of the battle. The admiral signals to the battleships that follow behind and repeats the memorable phrase "England expects each of us to do his duty".

I was truly impressed by that wonderful canvas, and in talking
with its outstanding artist we reminisced about the meeting at the
Strait. I think it will go down in history as a symbol of how far we
have come. As the launching pad of a new era, it must get the recognition it deserves. If Rivadavia could send photos of the Argentine
ships and an explanation of their position at the time the battleships
came face to face, as well as any other details he deems necessary,
De Martino could sketch out the scene. The government would then
use that sketch to prepare the final canvas. If my idea is acceptable
to you, please let me know or inform Rivadavia of your wishes. As
far as I am concerned there are many reasons why it would be beneficial for a piece of art to preserve that historic moment. This far-
reaching event has yet to be fully comprehended.

Yours truly,

FRANCISCO P. MORENO

Note: The Royal Society, the most highly regarded scientific soci-ety in England, has requested that I present the large photos of Patagonia at its annual public forum on the 21st of this month. The purpose of the photo exhibit is to give members a better idea of what these territories are like. Five hundred square feet of space, or more if necessary will be provided. The Patagonian landscape is garner-ing a lot of attention these days.

In 1902 Moreno found himself in Nahuel Huapi again, act-ing as expert adviser for the Argentine government and host-ing the British arbiter, Colonel Sir Thomas Holdich. In a telegram he sent to the President of Argentina, Lieutenant General Julio A. Roca, he wrote:

Lieutenant General Julio A. Roca[50]
President of the Argentine Republic
Buenos Aires

SIR: Allow me to say that I would much appreciate it if you could defer any decisions involving lands or forests in these remote territories until my return at the beginning of June. I would like to remind you of the pleasant discussion we had the day of my depar-ture. You agreed with me regarding those issues and I must say that it would be perfectly feasible to turn this region into an affluent area in less than two years. For your information, Holdich shares my views, but please do not discuss this with anyone. We will travel through the Cordillera from October 14 to 16. I am happy to report that I am doing well. Take care, my friend,
  Yours truly,
  FRANCISCO P. MORENO
  Nahuel Huapi, April 12, 1902

[50] From Emilio E. Frey's own handwritten copy. A friend of Moreno's, he was an engineer, and a loyal collaborator during the border dispute with Chile. He was the first superintendent of Nahuel Huapi National Park and an enthusiastic promoter of Nahuel Huapi for many years prior to that.

Little did Moreno know that eighteen months later on November 6, 1903, he would be donating to the Nation the core parcel that was later expanded and set aside as the magnificent Nahuel Huapi National Park.[51] Neither did he suspect that his request to Minister José Francisco Vergara would have repercussions in Chile, where a national park was subsequently created bordering ours in Argentina.

As the years went by, Moreno remained interested in Patagonian affairs, but was forced to redirect his efforts towards other initiatives. Then, in 1912, the ex-president of the United States of America, Colonel Theodore Roosevelt, who was visiting southern Argentina, asked Moreno to wait for him in Nahuel Huapi upon his return from Chile. So Moreno returned to that region one last time to hear his friend, the North American political leader, talk about national park policies and their significance. As a leader of the conservation movement in North America, Roosevelt had been personally involved in saving these important natural resorces.

In the years since that unforgettable visit to Nahuel Huapi, Moreno never relented in his attempts to convince the authorities of the need to concern themselves with land issues and land use. He was aware of the neglect to which our natural resources were being subjected. Yet no matter how often he voiced his concerns throughout the country, people rarely listened. Therefore, on July 30, 1917, he welcomed the opportunity to do something for his homeland in the belief that this time he would achieve some success. He wrote a long memorandum to the Minister of Agriculture, Dr. Honorio Pueyrredón, suggesting what could and should be done to improve the situation in these territories.

Moreno summed it up in the following terms, "I now con-

---

[51] From the original text that mentions the donation of the initial core of Nahuel Huapi National Park (See Appendix).

clude this hastily written memorandum, and have decided to expand it into a book with illustrations. I have written about events I personally experienced, and did so out of concern for our national interests. Now that my work is done, I would like to reflect upon it. At the beginning I checked maps of our territories and those of our neighbors, but now that it is over I see the global picture. As I ponder over the powerful economic forces that shaped other nations and how these could add to or detract from our own growth, I cannot help but insist upon the urgent need to develop our resources in order to avoid the deleterious effects emerging foreign interests could have on our country's future.

Cattle raising is becoming a common enterprise in Bolivia, Paraguay, and Brazil. Brazil is also a grain-producing country. Very soon its cattle industry will be competing with ours. Further north, in Colombia and Venezuela, the cattle business will soon benefit from more favorable conditions. Sheepherding is also expanding in Perú, Ecuador, and Bolivia, as I mentioned. Canada's farming industry has reached the same production levels as ours, while South Africa is advancing rapidly. In Asia, once the war is over (1914-1918), no matter who wins it, only Mesopotamia and Asia Minor will be capable of producing more grain than we do, with the added advantage of their close proximity to large population centers. Meanwhile, Siberia is on its way to becoming the future breadbasket of the world, and the colossal growth of its cattle-raising industry should not be underestimated. In 1893 not a single pound of butter was exported from this region. Twenty years later, butter exports surpassed the forty thousand ton mark!

Let us not delude ourselves thinking we will continue to be rated among the leading producers of grain, meat, wool and leather based on our current productive capacity. We must think in terms of increasing production many times fold, and we will manage to do so once we develop wise land management policies.

It will take the work of a large-scale institution to bring

about a major increase in production. Such an organization would conduct soil reports, land-use feasibility studies, and official land surveys, while scrutinizing all land grants to private industry in order to protect the public interest from any possible negative impact these concessions might have. In all likelihood this would have to be an umbrella institution encompassing the Bureau of Land Management, the General Mining and Geology Office, and the National Forest and Grassland Service. It would carry out technical studies of land and water resources, while all administrative duties would be handled by administrative subdivisions. The executive government should not find it too hard to find skilled persons of good will who would make up a commission to determine the viability of this proposal. Once the geographic conditions, physical environment, and potential of our soil are assessed, a plan can be drawn up.

Let us start a movement like the one presidents Theodore Roosevelt and William Taft spearheaded in the United States. We should emulate them and seek ways to manage our natural resources without exhausting them. We will then be in a position to generate the wealth that will save the Republic from its current hard times. We still own vast tracts of good public lands. If we allocate the small amount of money needed to fund the institution's preliminary studies, we will reap millions in fiscal revenues, not just the few hundred pesos that the government now draws. For example, it is unbelievable that areas that feed only 1,000 sheep are leased at the same rate as those where 6,000 graze. Never underestimate the ignorance of those who dole out land grants. This wasteful disregard for our resources is a fast road to ruin.

In my letter to the Minister of Agriculture, dated this past May 28, I urged him to stop all coal and petroleum concessions. In 1907, President Roosevelt permanently set aside one hundred million acres in his country as national land, given the petroleum, coal, and mineral deposits the acreage contained. Let us do the same with those lands of ours that are rich in these resources. Beware of those who hoard them for commercial or political gain! The national government should also officially declare the water supply –torrents and waterfalls included– to be in national ownership. Above all, we must study the land, as common sense dictates. Current laws and non-scientific methods must be changed. That is the only way we will ever become the "Great American Nation of the South."

Moreno died on November 22, 1919, two years after writing this memorandum. Although he felt he had been forgotten, he never stopped dreaming of a "great fatherland, great among the greatest," and of the bright future of his beloved Patagonia. He was also concerned for the welfare of the Indians and their descendants, among them, the children of the arrogant Cacique Valentín Shaihueque, with whom he had exchanged a friendly handshake back in 1876.

APPENDIX

PART III

I

TEXT OF THE LETTER FOR THE DONATION OF THE CORE PARCEL DESIGNATED AS NAHUEL HUAPI NATIONAL PARK

Buenos Aires, November 6, 1903

Your Excellency, Minister of Agriculture,
Dr. Wenceslao Escalante

Dear Sir:

Law No. 4192, enacted and published in the Official Bulletin of the Nation this past August 2, declares that I shall be awarded an extension of public lands located in Neuquén or South of the Río Negro. This honor is bestowed upon me for the services I rendered to my country prior to being designated as Argentina's Expert (Perito) in the demarcation of the border with Chile.

During the years I devoted to my explorations, when I went off to the southern territories to pursue the work that later prompted this honor, I was treated to the most beautiful scenery my eyes had ever seen. On several occasions I explained why it would be in our nation's best interest to hold on to some of these beautiful places for the benefit of current and future generations, following the example of the United States and other countries that have magnificent unspoiled parkland. Today, Legislation 4192 allows me to take possession of the same stretch of territory where many years ago I could glimpse future greatness. At that time, the lands were unknown and disputed, but through their exploration and study, they were consolidated under Argentine ownership.

I take much pleasure in coming forward today to make a donation that will help make the dreams of a lifetime come to fruition.

I am here to request, pursuant to the law, that a three-square-league area located betv een Neuquén and Río Negro be designated as a nature reserve. This region lies at the western edge of the main fiord off Nahuel Huapi lake. I ask that on behalf of the nation you accept this donation. It extends from an area encompassing Laguna de los Cántaros to the north and reaches the Barros Arana gap to the south while being flanked on its western border with Chile by the Raulíes and Pérez Rosales gaps. On its eastern border there is a mountain range rising to the east of Ensenada de Puerto Blest and Laguna Frías. It includes the most interesting array of natural wonders I have ever seen in Patagonia. Every time I visited this region I told myself that if it was ever set aside as public land by inalienable right it would soon grow into a great center for intellectual and social activities and become a catalyst for human advancement. The physical and natural phenomena that one observes there are beginning to attract scholars who would be perfectly happy conducting research amid the natural splendor of lakes, torrents, vast forests, steep mountains, and permafrost. Geographically, this unmatched area defies description. Together with Australia, New Zealand, and Europe, this territory, washed by the waters of the Atlantic, is uniquely suited to the purpose of the donation I am now making. This land of beauty in the Andes is home to a colossal peak shared by two nations: Monte Tronador unites both of them. Chile also has public lands in the area and may decide to preserve them as well. In that way, the inhabitants of both sides of the Andes could marvel in the magnificent tranquility and serene beauty of the countryside. Together, they could rest and share ideas there; they could find solutions to problems unsolved by diplomacy. Visitors from around the world would mingle and share with one another at this international crossroads. Natural progress would reap the benefits of this geographically privileged area in the Southern hemisphere. In making the donation I wish that the landscape be preserved in its current state and that development of this plot be reduced to the minimum necessary to accommodate cultured visitors to its sanctuary. Their presence will always be beneficial to the region that has finally come under our sovereignty. Its growth must be rapid but care-

*fully planned so that it can lead Argentina forward in a manner
consistent with our nation's goals.*

It is an honor and a pleasure to address you.

Sincerely yours,

FRANCISCO F. MORENO

This donation was accepted through the following presidential decree:

Buenos Aires, February 1, 1904

*In view of the present offer and recognizing the significance of
these lands in terms of their location and that Doctor Moreno hereby expressly renounces ownership of three leagues granted to him
so that they can be designated as National Parkland;*

The President of the Argentine Republic

ORDERS:

*Article 1. That his offer to relinquish ownership shall be accepted and that said area should be reserved as National Parkland and
precluded from any possible concession to private parties.*

*Article 2. That Dr. Moreno shall be given notice of this executive
decree and that he shall be thanked.*

ROCA
W. Escalante

In 1916, by executive decree dated May 26, Mr. Jorge Newbery, a man who inhabited the region, was appointed commissioner of this natural reserve in charge of setting up The
National Park of the South, a position he took ad-honorem.

INDEX

Other works published
by El Elefante Blanco

Esta edición
de 1000 ejemplares
se terminó de imprimir en
A.B.R.N. Producciones Gráficas S.R.L.,
Wenceslao Villafañe 468,
Buenos Aires, Argentina,
en enero de 2003.